Dance with me in the Heart

The adults' guide to great infant-parent partnerships

Pennie Brownlee

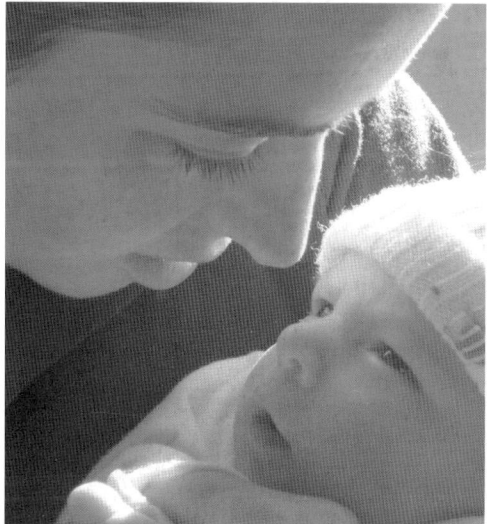

Also by Pennie Brownlee:
Magic Places: The Adults' Guide to Young Children's Creative Art Work.

Publishing History

2008 - Playcentre Publications Limited, New Zealand
2014 - Revised edition, Ako Books - NZ Playcentre Publications
2016 - Revised edition, Good Egg Books

Reprinted 2009, 2010, 2013, 2015

Copyright © Pennie Brownlee 2008, 2014, 2016

ISBN: 978-0-473-36146-4

A catalogue record for this book is available from the National Library of New Zealand.

Design and layout: Pennie Brownlee
Printed by T L Print, Auckland, New Zealand
Published by Good Egg Books, Thames, New Zealand

good egg books

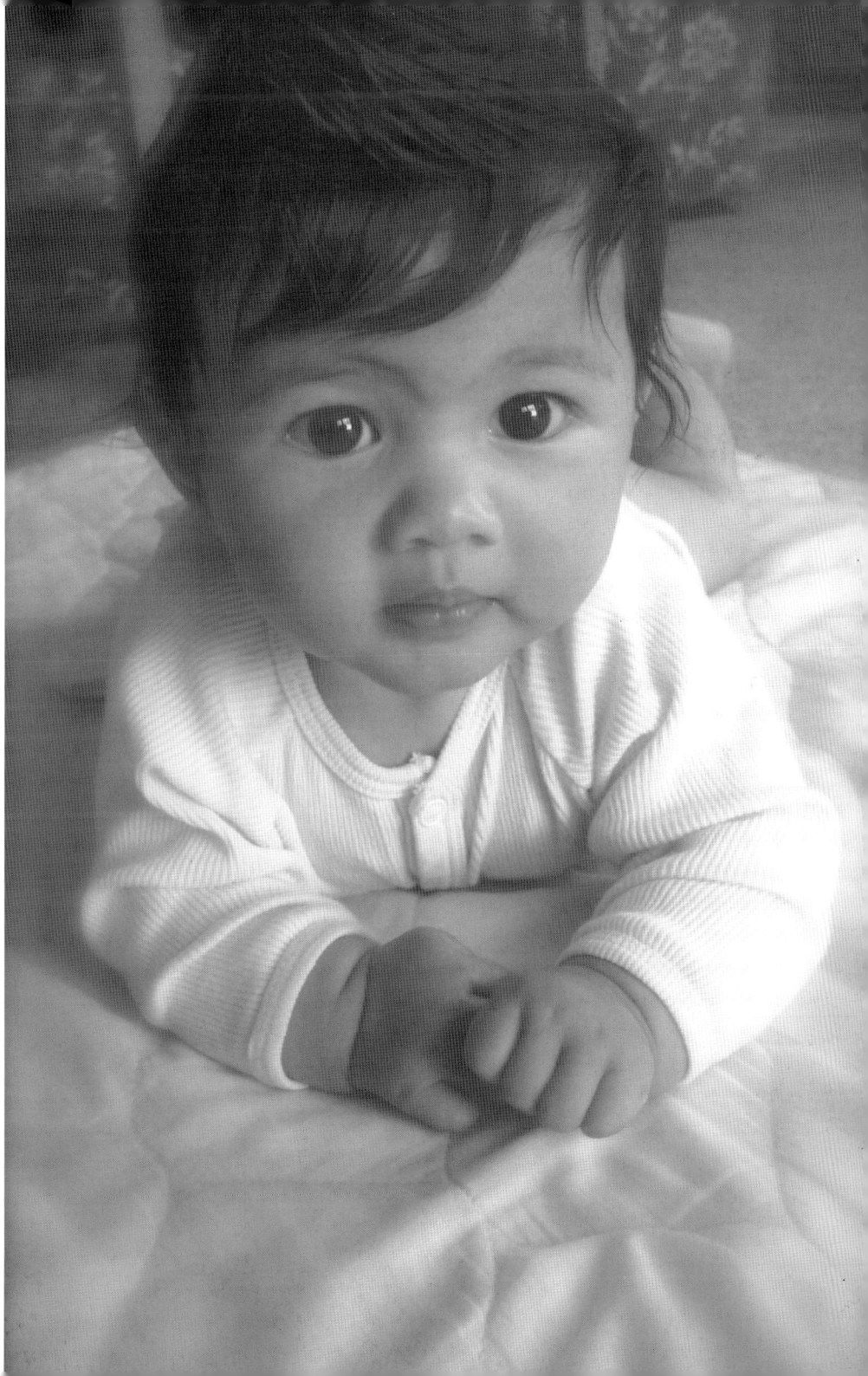

Dance with me in the Heart · Contents

To Mum, Clare, Scarlett and Olivia, with much love.

The invitation

Every baby begins life in a partner dance with her mother. The partnership of creation we call pregnancy is the first part of the partner dance. Already a partner-on-the-inside, each baby is expecting to continue the partner dance when birth delivers her to the outside world. Indeed, she is genetically programmed for the continuation of that first partnership, and she brings two steps into her new life; two skills which enable her creation dance to continue. She will offer 'invitations' to her parents to partner her based on her deepest needs, and she will accept her parents' invitations for partnership based on their needs. The invitation opens the heart space to peaceful partnership. Throughout the pages of this book you will find clues and tips to assist you in creating a great partnership with your baby.

Problem pronouns

When referring to babies in the English language, we use the singular pronouns *he, she* and *it*. Most people use *it* when they are talking about babies, and I used to too. *It* is the pronoun for things and not for people. Using *it* takes away the baby's humanity and that is an invitation to abuse. While we use *it* for babies we would never use *it* for adults, it doesn't sound right: *The adult stopped its bike. It took some bread from its bag and it threw it out for the ducks.*

So that only leaves *he* and *she*, and they are gendered. People say that if we use *he* everyone knows that means *he* and *she*. The research does not support this. It seems we perceive the gender suggested by the pronoun. So rather than leave the girls out altogether, I have tried to give boy babies and girl babies their equal share.

Introduction

This book is the result of years of being: being a Mum, being a Playcentre Mum, and being alongside adults and children in a learning setting for forty-plus years now. Equally as important, I have been marinated in the ideas of brilliant people. Much of my thinking is the result of being able to access their research and wisdom through their books, and through their courses. There will be a bibliography at the back to acknowledge these people, and to point you in their direction for the fuller picture.

Two people stand out: Joseph Chilton Pearce, whom I have followed since I read his book *Magical Child* in the early 1980s, and the late Dr Emmi Pikler whom I only 'met' in 2004 when I attended the first summer school in the English language at the Pikler Institute in Budapest. Both of them are, to my way of thinking, geniuses who show the way to the end of societal violence. They both understand that the key to a peaceful future lies in the infant-adult relationship.

If you haven't 'met' these two people before, I would love to introduce you to them and their ideas, as best I can. I can only give you my take on their ideas and hope that my take is near to the spirit of their work. Both of them direct you back to your baby. Both of them understood that the cues your baby gives you will choreograph your successful dance partnership.

"If you are really going to co-operate with Nature's plan for the development of intelligence, you take your signals from the child. Not from a book, not from an expert, not from a tape. You take your signals from the child."
Joseph Chilton Pearce

"What is important is that we learn what is essential. What is essential is to observe! Get to know your child. If you really recognise what your child needs, if you feel what is causing him grief, feel what she needs, then you will respond in the right way. You will guide and bring up your child well."
Dr Emmi Pikler

It starts at the beginning

I am the oldest. When my Mother had me she loved me dearly. I can see that in the photo, but I'm glad I have the photo because Mum and I got off on the wrong foot right from the beginning. We were out of step when I was new, and once that out-of-step pattern was established, we pretty much danced like that until I left home.

My brother is a year and a week younger than I am and Mum absolutely adored him, but she got off on the wrong foot with him too. Mum was new to the job of parenting and she didn't trust her own feelings and instincts about loving and caring for her babies. She didn't trust herself, or us, enough to read our cues and dance with us, which is weird because our Mum was a truly fantastic dancer. I guess she just hadn't thought that she could have a dance partnership with her babies. Instead, she followed the advice of Plunket, with its since-discarded four-hourly-feeding-and-don't-pick-them-up-in-between routine, to the letter. My Mum was going to be the very best Mum and that is why she did what 'the expert' told her to do. To the letter.

A peace declaration

It didn't work. Years later Mum told us of her anguish when Bruce was screaming and obviously hurting and hungry but her 'not being allowed' to pick him up. So when our sister Sue was born four and a half years after Bruce, Mum made the famous declaration: *"I'm not fighting with this baby*

1

over feeding, sleeping, toilet training ... anything. This baby can eat what she likes, when she likes, as much as she likes, as little as she likes, sleep when she likes, sleep as long as she likes." My Mother had declared peace. She was going to take her signals from her child. And Mum really enjoyed Sue, right from the word go. They grew a partnership, a most satisfying dance for both of them. Tellingly, Sue is Mum's only child whom she breast-fed, and her only child whom she neither screamed at nor hit. Mum was in right relationship with Sue from the beginning.

The world has changed since then
You can tell by the photo that Mum was learning to be a parent a long time ago, more than sixty years ago in fact, and the world has changed a lot in sixty years. Not very much is the same as it was then: not the clothes, the cars, the telephones nor the food. There were no computers, CAT scanners, MRI scanners, no internet or many of the other wonders that have helped us learn more about babies and their parents.

Some things haven't changed
In relation to babies, there are two things that haven't changed. Babies themselves haven't changed. Babies are still the same babies, with the same design, the same needs and the same potential as way back then. Here in New Zealand our ideas about what is good for babies hasn't changed much since then either. Even some trained health and education professionals are still giving out the same kind of misinformation as was given to my Mother over sixty years ago, and advice from friends and family can be equally damaging and behind the times.

We are luckier than my Mum because there now is a wealth of research available to us; research which underscores the importance of the beginning - the early partnership between the parent and the baby. It validates all parents who tune in to their baby, and who follow what *feels* right. These parents follow their hearts, literally, because it turns out that it is the heart that leads us in the elegant dance between infant and adult.

The heart

Three wishes

If your baby could tell you what she would really like from you, she would tell you that she would like three wishes: to feel safe, to feel loved and to be respected. She wouldn't care in which order her wishes were granted, but she would definitely ask for all three. Any one wish by itself is not enough; it is only part of the parcel. She would know that the granting of those three wishes would allow her to learn how to dance with you in the heart again, the same as she did before she was born into this new-to-her world. That is what she wants with all her heart.

Heart music

Every dance needs music and the heart provides the music for the dance between mothers - and fathers - and their babies. When your baby was in the womb there was never silence - it was noisy in there. There were all the sounds coming from the outside, sounds like your voice and the music you listened to, and there were the rumblings and the gurglings of your insides. But by far the most important sound to your baby was the constant beating of your heart. That drumbeat of Life was the constant music from conception to birth.

Every baby is designed to listen out for that heart-music as soon as she is born. When the baby comes up onto the mother's breast straight after birth and hears again that familiar music, every cell in her tiny body rejoices. Every cell tells the baby "Relax, you are home, you have made it safely through the birth journey. You can stop producing the hormones you needed for such an exacting physical performance and you can start getting to know your mother, from the outside."

Rhythm divine

Not only does your heart provide the beat for the dance, it also provides the rhythms. Your heart is truly the music that sets the dance between you, and there have been amazing discoveries recently which confirm what poets and lovers have always known: two hearts can beat as one.

3

Basic heart knowing

We have known for a long time that the heart is the pump which moves blood around our bodies. Recent discoveries from neurocardiology (*neuro* - brain, *cardio* - heart) have shown that our heart is also a 'brain' complete with neurons, or brain cells. The heart has its own intelligence. This intelligence is the Choreographer behind all successful partner dances, including your dance with your baby.

In addition to being a pump and having its own brain, your heart generates the largest source of rhythmic electromagnetic energy in your body. It has an electromagnetic field that carries information about what you are feeling at any given moment. You may know that your heartbeat and rhythms can be measured with an electrocardiograph (ECG), but you might not know that scientists are now able to measure the electromagnetic field your heart generates. It is strongest up to one metre from your heart and they suspect it goes much further, in all directions. Of course your baby knows this field well because she grew in it in the womb. At the same time, she grew her own heart and its own electromagnetic field. There are no prizes for guessing whose heart is the strongest and whose has the most influence for the early years of the baby's life.

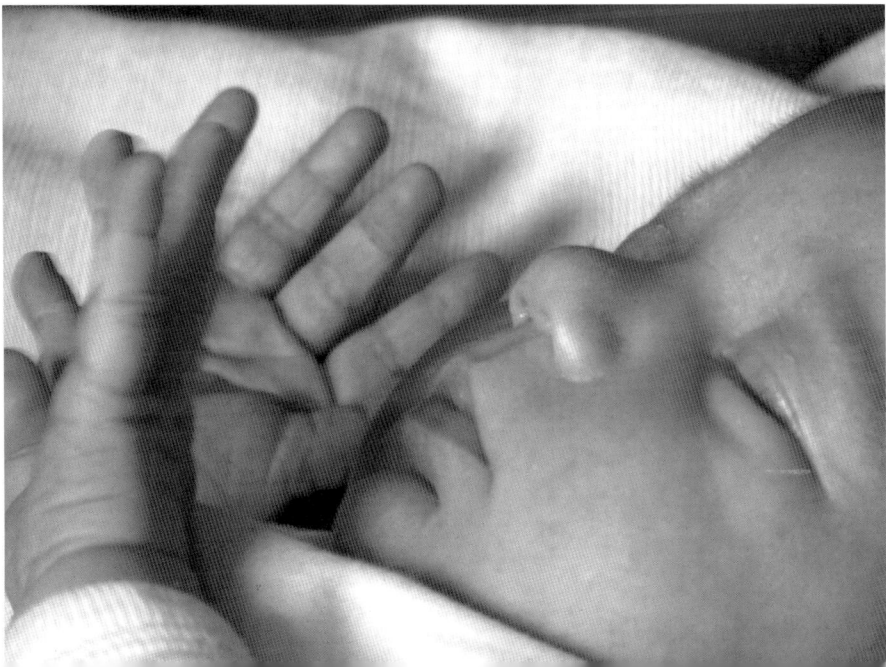

You are the senior dance partner

You act like a tuning fork for your baby. That is fine if you are relaxed - it means you will have a baby who is relaxed too. But what if you are stressed? Your baby will 'match' stress too, she cannot do any differently because you *are* the senior partner.

You choose

As adults we can choose to be stressed or not. Babies cannot make that choice; they are dependent on what the senior dance partner is choosing. It doesn't matter which method you choose to stay peaceful, even simple things like the music you are listening to will affect your heart and brain rhythms causing peace or stress. Some people meditate to destress, others prefer to have a long hot bath, others stop and pay attention to their breathing. Choose anything that works for you. Relaxation takes you to the doorway of your heart, grace and positive emotions usher you in.

Heart and brain together

The brain is also an electromagnetic generator and receiver, though its frequencies are feeble compared to the much stronger frequencies of your heart. There is a state when both heart and brain frequencies come into alignment, and this state is called *heart coherence*. It is the exact opposite of stress. You know when you are in heart coherence - you feel calm, relaxed and peaceful, yet energised, focused and clear. When you stand there looking at the miracle of your sleeping baby and you feel your heart warm and peaceful - that is a good dose of heart coherence.

No-stress dancing

Imagine if you were learning a new dance and the dancing partner who was teaching you was stressed and uptight, it would be hard for you to stay relaxed. It wouldn't be much fun either. But if your dancing partner was very relaxed and laid back it would be a much more successful venture. You would enjoy the dancing and each other; you would be in heart coherence. That is probably the most important part of the partner dance sequence we can learn: to get into heart coherence at will.

Choose the heart

Researchers at the Institute of HeartMath have shown that you need to generate a positive emotion, like the love you have for your baby, to create and sustain heart coherence. When you choose heart coherence it also ensures *your* health and happiness. If you are feeling stress, anxiety or frustration, your heart rhythm pattern is incoherent, whereas if you are feeling love, compassion, appreciation or gratitude, your heart rhythm is coherent.

Heart habit

HeartMath has developed scientifically validated ways for adults (and children) to train themselves to get into heart coherence whenever they choose. They even have computer software and computerised hand-held devices to assist you as you make being in heart coherence a habit. These programs measure your heart variability rate and show you when your heart rhythm patterns go from stress or incoherence, to coherence. Whether you choose to use any of the age-old ways of staying in the heart or the newest technological wizardry, it is the most important part of the dance. If you are not in the heart the partnership is off to a very shaky start.

Baby can teach you

If you truly intend to get into the heart then, paradoxically, your baby can help you to do that. We will look at how that happens as we go along.

The stories

Dancing with the stars

If you were to be invited to appear on *Dancing with the Stars*, you would hope that your senior dancing partner believed you were an intelligent human being who would be able to learn to dance well and partner them elegantly. That way the two of you would have a chance. Well if babies could talk, they would tell you they hope for exactly the same when they land here in the Earth Dance. It really matters what beliefs we hold about each other - these 'stories' decide how we think and behave. Thinking and behaving turn the stories into the real thing.

We can choose our stories

Here is an example from one of the people I admire, Mark Inglis. He lost his legs to frostbite. He could have had this story in his head, *"I haven't got any legs now so that is pretty much it for me,"* and settled into a wheel-chair with the TV remote. Plenty do do that, but not him. He chose to create another story altogether, one which saw him dance very differently, all the way up Mt Everest and back again.

What we believe creates our world, including how we are with our babies, and in New Zealand we have some beliefs about babies and children which are past their use-by date. These negative beliefs need to be discarded for beliefs which enable us to stay in the heart.

7

Horror stories

It is a good idea to stop every so often and see how we are doing as a country. That way we can see if we like where we are heading, or whether we need to change course a bit to end up where we want to be. As I write, New Zealand is currently bottom out of the OECD countries for child abuse, neglect and fatalities. We probably are not 'comparing apples with apples' in that it is unlikely that every country has equivalent reporting procedures. What is really distressing though is that every year our statistics are worsening. The statistics are the tip of the iceberg: they only tell of the reported incidents from the categories of abuse that are reportable. They don't even hint at the levels of violence considered 'normal' in our culture.

The Naughty story

We have the story that children are naughty, and boy children are even naughtier. You hear this story all the time: *"You naughty naughty little boy."* We haven't stopped to ask whether this is a true story or a self-fulfilling fiction because we 'know' it is a true story. But what if it isn't? What if it only turns out to be true because we *believe* it is a true story, so we think and act it out?

One of the great benefits of living in these times is that we can look at how other cultures treat their babies and children. We can learn what stories they hold about children, we can observe the reality that results from their stories. Some cultures do worse than we are doing, but many do far better and we can learn a lot from them. The Yequana Indians of the Venezuelan jungle do not have the Naughty story. They don't even have a word for naughty, or a word for disobedient. Naughty and disobedient simply do not exist; they have never heard of them. They think this is normal, and for them it is. Without the *idea* of naughty or disobedient, without the *words* naughty and disobedient, without the *story* of naughtiness and disobedience there is none to be found.

We can do better than naughty

It is time to have a good look at our stories and see which ones we could leave behind. The Naughty story would be a great place to start. The Blank-Slate story, Born in Original Sin, Unreliable, Incapable and Helpless stories have all had their time and they need to go. It would be great if we could just call up the old stories on our 'brain-screen' and delete them, but we can't. Stories have a tighter grip on us than that. When it comes to parting with negative stories it takes vigilance until we have the new story in place. We need to listen very carefully to what we are thinking and to what words we are using. Our thoughts, words and deeds will tell us whether we are still acting out the old stories or not.

War stories

One of the old stories you hear over and over is the Baby as Adversary story. People who hold this story to be true think that the baby is out to get them. You can hear it in what they say:

He is only having you on.
Don't go in there, that will only reward her for being naughty.
He is playing you up.
If you listen to that you'll make a rod for your own back.
You have to show him who's boss, early.
Don't let her rule the roost.
It's either you or him.
Put her at the other end of the house so you can't hear her cry. That'll teach her.
Your are spoiling him. You're going to regret it.

These are not stories that promote heart coherence, these are baby-battling stories and they promote stress. Stress for the parents and the baby.

Baby-battlers

There are basically two ways you can play it with your baby: you can see the baby as a cunning adversary and become a baby-battler, or you can view your baby as a divine child and work for a partnership. Baby-battlers probably do not even realise that they are at war with babies because baby-battling is such a common phenomenon in New Zealand culture. If you were brought up in New Zealand you are almost sure to have caught a good dose of baby-battling disease. Fortunately there is a good recovery rate once you start to recognise the signs of the illness and begin to change the way you think.

Of this I am sure: baby-battlers, like my Mum was, love and care for their babies dearly. They just haven't been given an up-to-date picture of infant and child development so they don't know that some of the things they believe about babies are actually not possible. For example, it is not possible for an infant to 'play you up', to 'have you on', or to be naughty. Baby-battlers just misinterpret all the cues to match their view of babies. They are also not aware that some of the things they think are good for babies are in fact damaging. But with new stories about babies, baby-battlers can and do change. They learn to dance the partnership dance like my Mum did.

Off by heart stories
What we need are stories that are worthy of our babies and children. Equally important, we need stories about our children that are worthy of us. These stories will always be centred in the heart, and we will explore these stories when we look at care, development and play.

Every Baby is The Divine Child
Every Child is a Miracle
Every Child is Born Capable
Every Child is a Free and Equal Human Being
Every Child is Born to Act Out the Love Story
Every Child Wants to Dance in the Heart

The brain

The basic dance is three years long

With improved technologies, scientists are beginning to uncover secrets about how a baby's brain grows and develops. What they have discovered is that the initial critical time for your baby's brain is while he is still in the womb. Well that makes sense because that is when the brain is growing. But a baby is born before the basics in the brain are grown. If the baby stayed in the womb until the brain had laid down the basics he would be in there for eighteen months. That doesn't bear thinking about. Therefore, the second critical period of brain development is the first year of life, and scientists have come to the consensus that it is all critical until the baby reaches his third birthday. By critical they mean that what happens in those three years will become the foundation for everything which follows. Everything. The connections will be made - or not made - and the patterns will be set.

Stress is not good for growing brains

When the baby is in the womb it is the emotional state of the mother which decides how her baby's brain develops. An emotional state in humans is not only an electromagnetic event of frequencies, it is a molecular event as well. Hormones, or chemical messengers, are flooded through the body and their role is to regulate functions in the body. The baby in the womb gets his dose of his mother's molecules-of-emotion through the placenta. If a baby is flooded in the hormones of stress he puts his growth effort into the part of the brain which is designed to deal with stress and threat - the fight and flight part of his brain. He cannot do differently. That is what the chemical messengers dictate. If you were a baby in the womb and you had a choice between being marinated in the hormones of stress or the hormones of peacefulness, which one would you choose?

Heart coherence grows great brains

When the baby in the womb is marinated in the hormones which accompany heart coherence, then he is free to get on developing his higher brain structures. These are just the structures he will need for the highest human qualities like love, trust, beauty, respect, empathy and truth. These babies are already in the habit of peacefulness before they make their grand entrance into the world. That is the start every baby deserves, and it is why many cultures go to great lengths to nurture pregnant mothers. Being loved and nurtured keeps a mother-to-be from being stressed.

The tuning fork effect

Once the baby is out of the womb he no longer gets flooded with his mother's hormones, he makes his own. But he will make them according to his mother's emotional state, and he does this by 'matching' her heart-brain frequencies. You have probably seen this happen. You will have seen a baby who is really distressed, and his mother is also distressed and nothing she does seems to work to calm him down. Enter the baby's father (or his nanna) who takes the baby, and the baby calms down just like that. If they had one of those hand-held gadgets for reading heart coherence that I mentioned before, it is a sure bet that mum would have been out of coherence while dad would have been in coherence. The baby doesn't need a gadget though, he just matches the frequencies.

Holey brains

What scientists have discovered using brain scans on children who are three has really shaken up the world of early childhood. Children who have had almost non-stop stress - from abandonment, threat, violence, neglect or abuse - have huge holes in their higher brain structures. They don't have the hardware to run the software of peace and partnership. Instead, they have highly developed defensive brains for fight and flight. Highly developed defence-department-brains don't grow healthy partnerships, they lead to baby-battlers, violence and war. Scans of violent adults reveal the holes are still there - they don't repair themselves. It is in the first three years that the growth is laid down, or not.

Shall I hit you?

"Whoa!" I hear you saying to yourself, *"That is a random question out of nowhere."* In a way it is, and in a way it isn't. If you haven't developed the

parts of your higher brain which deal with *affect regulation* and you are really angry, you can't even *ask* that question. If that part of the brain is not there to call on, you will use your fight-flight brain instead. You have to - there is nothing else developed to deal with overwhelming emotions, so it's 'shoot first and ask questions later'. When the emotions have subsided, many many people deeply regret their actions - later. Even more tragic, there are some in our society who didn't even grow their capability for regret.

Holy brains

Babies who have been peacefully nurtured throughout their growing are very different. Their brains have huge prefrontal cortices. Researcher Paul MacLean termed this part of the brain the "angel lobes" because they are associated with the highest human qualities. These babies are perfectly set up for their divine birthright; the happiness that comes from loving and being loved. Remember at the beginning of this book we said that if your baby could tell you what she would really like from you, she wouldn't ask you for toys and things. She would tell you that she wanted to feel safe and loved, and now you can see why it is so important for her. Her future rests upon it.

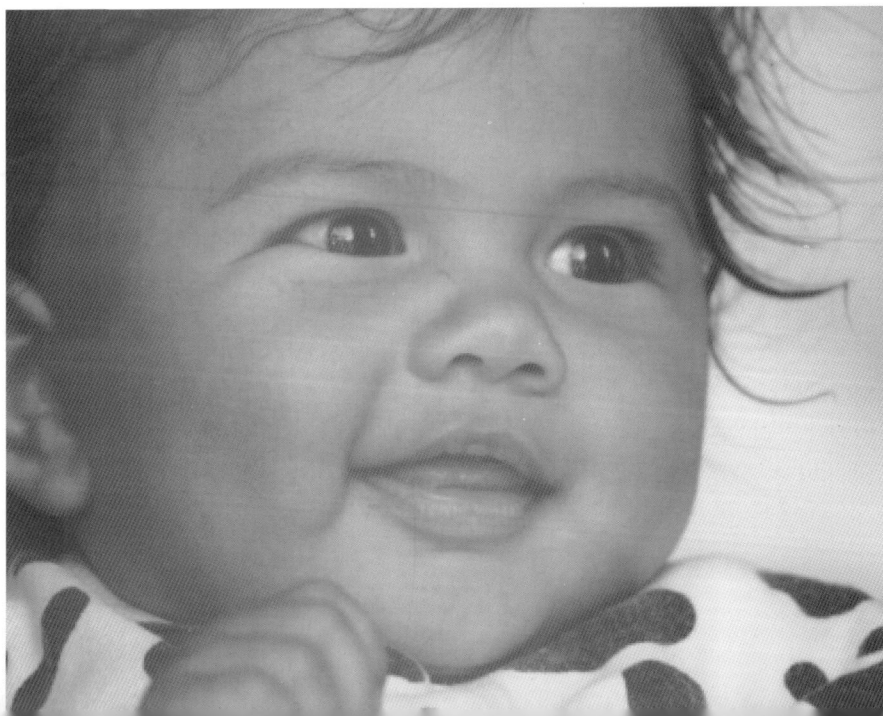

The First Partnership, naturally

Womb then mother
Stating the obvious, the womb provides everything the baby needs, it provides the nourishment and the environment for the baby to grow. Babies cannot grow outside of the womb. They can 'get started in a test tube', but they cannot grow into babies there. Baby mammals have to be grown in the womb. After the birth the mother provides everything the baby needs: this mother-baby couple is the First Partnership. It is from within *this* partnership that the baby learns to make relationships. From the safety and love of this first partnership the baby will move out to make relationships with dad, with brothers and sisters, nannas and poppas, aunts and uncles. That is why in cultures that do well by their children, the mother and baby are both cared for and nurtured together.

Nurture the mother-baby partnership
Wise cultures are child-wise, and child-wise cultures do everything they can to ensure the mother and the baby get off to the best start in those first three years. They understand the health of their culture depends on it. It's not hard to see why either. If the baby has a bonded relationship with mum he grows heart-brain connections for the highest human qualities and so is able to make peaceful relationships with everyone else in the group.

Bonded together
This first partnership needs to be grown from the moment of birth, and people refer to this partnering as *bonding* and *attachment*. Both the mother and the baby come complete with all that is needed to make the perfect partnership, but the conditions have to be right. If they are not, these inbuilt abilities are not activated and the partnership can fail. We are going to look at some of the conditions which act like the super-glue for the mother-baby bond.

Natural birth
Not surprisingly, a calm and easy natural birth is the best start you could hope for, and one which almost every mother can manage, as long as they get the right support. The trick is tracking down the right support.

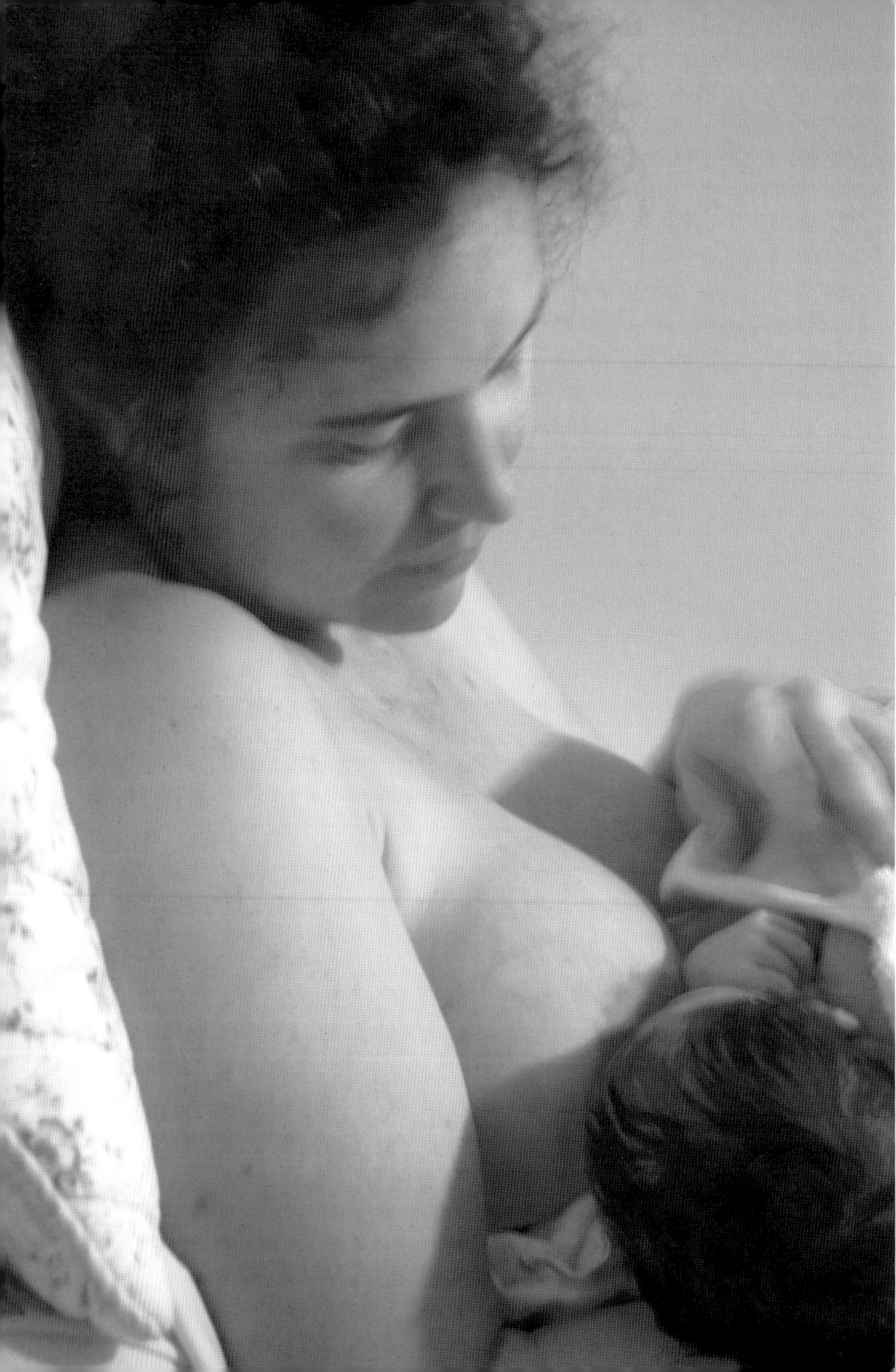

Birthing has been taken over by the medical profession which has gone way beyond the necessary and valued role as back-up should something untoward happen. With their foetal monitors and elective caesarians, a natural process has been turned into a medical-entertainment phenomenon with the mother sidelined as a bystander, watching her baby on a screen. Her baby is not out there on a screen, her baby is *in her.* Her consciousness needs to be centred *in* her body, co-driving the birth process, not outside of her body, absent from the 'driver's seat'.

The mother births
Since we are mammals we have mammalian needs to facilitate the safe and normal birthing we are designed for. Most mammals make safe 'nests' when left to do it their way; they go away and birth by themselves. In the case of the larger mammals like whales and elephants, they have one or more 'skilled midwives' in attendance. We, like they, need a quiet peaceful place, subdued lighting, and most importantly, as little interference as possible. We do far better with a skilled midwife (who appreciates that the medical model is there as back-up), than with attendants whose only training is medical. Skilled midwives, like their elephant and whale counterparts, have given birth themselves and they know and trust the ancient codings in the mother's body. They know how to support the normal process of birth. Their heart coherence in this situation is just what the birthing mother needs to stay in coherence herself, and to allow her body-intelligence to complete the mystery of bringing a new baby into the world.

The midwife supports
If things in the environment are out of alignment with the mother's deep and ancient needs, her body stops the birthing process. It's designed to. It's part of that ancient safety mechanism in the brain designed to protect the mother and her new baby. Drugs, bright lights, monitors and examinations are read by the mother's body-intelligence as unwelcome interference and her hormonal messengers automatically slow or stop the process until conditions return to favourable. For most women in the hospital setting the conditions do not approach 'desirable-for-mammals', and New Zealand's

growing rate of emergency caesarians is the evidence.

Breast feeding - there's a knack to it

Not surprisingly, the milk that the mother makes is just right for the baby: elephant milk is just right for baby elephants, seal milk for seals pups, cow's milk for calves and your milk is just right for your baby. While elephants and seals seem to feed first-off by instinct, sometimes we humans need some support to get started successfully nourishing our babies. Once again, the stories we hear can help or hinder so seek out the people who *know* the breast feeding story, and seek them out *really early* if things are not going as you and your baby want them. Ask your skilled midwife, ask to see a lactation specialist - don't be put off by that name - or seek out your nearest La Leche League. These women know that successful breast feeding is the best start for your partnership, and they also know how to put you at ease while they assist you to acquire the knack. That is their job.

I've got my eyes on you

After your baby has been born, come up onto your breast and heard your heartbeat, he or she looks at your face. Your newborn baby can keep your face in focus if you are at a distance of between 20 to 30 centimetres, just the distance of a baby feeding at the breast. This is probably not an accident of design, more likely it is another clue that things are much more complex than we have previously recognised. Your baby is actually programmed with the need to look into your face many times a day and night in that first year, and they gaze at you when they are feeding. The pattern of your face is the key their brain is waiting for; it activates development in the higher structures we have already mentioned. Frequent feeding not only feeds your baby's body, it also 'feeds' your baby's heart and brain.

What's in it for you Mum?

Frequent feeding means your brain delivers to you frequent doses of the hormones prolactin and oxytocin. Prolactin has been termed the mothering hormone - it accesses your mothering 'program'. Oxytocin is known as the love hormone: it is made and delivered wherever there is love. Both hormones can also bring about heart coherence, freedom from stress. That's just the kind of help any senior dance partner can do with. Interestingly, both mother and baby are awash in these two hormones for the hour after a natural peaceful birth. That hour is the time to literally 'fall in love' - it gives the partnership dance the start it deserves.

Partnership head start
To summarise: a peaceful pregnancy, a natural birth and breast feeding are keys to getting your baby-parent partnership underway. But what if you haven't managed to achieve one or all of these? What if your baby and you didn't get the ideal start, is it too late? Is there any hope for the perfect partnership for the both of you? Of course there is hope, there is always hope. The babies at the Pikler Institute have shown us just how much hope there is if we start where we are, and stop worrying about that which we cannot alter, that which might have been.

There's always hope
The babies at the Pikler Institute do not get the ideal start. Not only do they almost always miss out on the peaceful pregnancy, natural birth and breast feeding, they end up at the Institute because they have been abandoned and/or abused and then rescued by the State. They could hardly have a worse beginning, and yet in next to no time at all, they are in perfect partnership with the adults there, and their little lives are mending at the very deepest levels. In many ways, these unlucky babies are very lucky. These babies have landed with people who know exactly what to do to grow a partnership with an infant, even a traumatised infant. They have worked out the simple things to do so that the babies will have their three wishes met. They know how to respect infants so that each child feels safe and feels loved. The adult and child are together in the heart, literally.

Granting baby's three wishes

First, a word of warning

If you, like the nurses at the Pikler Institute, learn to do the simple respectful practices which grow a partnership with your baby, you will be doing things differently from the way most people in New Zealand treat babies. Doing things differently can be a very real threat to others and can cause conflict. This seems to stem from the habit the subconscious mind has of categorising things into the opposites of right and wrong. If family, friends or professionals do things in different ways from you, well one of you has to be right and one of you must be wrong - and you can count on it, it isn't going to be them. But you have mindfully weighed up the pros and cons and you have set out on a different path. Yours is not The Right Path nor The Wrong Path, it is a Different Path which is right for you and your baby.

Be the change you want to see in the world

On your path you will not enter into the right-wrong game if you are in the business of granting wishes. You understand that you have chosen to do things differently so that you and your baby can stay in your heart space together. Treating those with different views respectfully, you will not try to change *them*, you will just go ahead 'being the change you want to see in the world'. They, however, might want to change you, and you might have to say, *"Please respect that I have chosen to do things differently, that's all."*

Safe, loved and respected

If you ask parents if they respect their babies they look at you funny. To start with it isn't a question that has been popped to them before, and mostly they have never thought about it. But it isn't such a silly question. A lot of the things we do to babies, with good intentions, are actually very disrespectful when you start thinking about them. Take picking up a baby without telling them, or worse, picking them up from behind when they don't know you are there. Imagine if someone did that to you, you would definitely get a fright, and you probably wouldn't feel safe or calm either, yet this happens to babies a lot.

Which steps will we be dancing?

When the baby is out of the womb absolutely everything is new to begin with, including every step of this partnership dance. *You* know what the steps are, *you* know what you intend, but your baby has no idea. Put yourself in the baby's shoes: if you were learning new steps from an expert, wouldn't you want them to let you know what was about to happen *before* it happened? And being a quick learner, you would eventually get to know from the cues given just what was going to happen. You would feel secure knowing what was coming, and so it is with the baby.

If you gently tell the baby what is going to happen before it happens, from day one, every time, it will not be long before your clever baby puts two and two together. He will work out what your cues signal, and he can begin to anticipate what will happen. When a baby can *anticipate* what will happen, he can *participate* in it when it happens, and the pair of you begin to dance together.

Follow me

So, if you are going to wash your baby's face with a face-cloth, you hold the face-cloth where your baby can see it, that way there are no surprises. You tell him softly, *"I am going to wash your face"*, and you wait a while. When you pause you allow him time to process all the cues you have given, then you go ahead and gently wash his face. If you are going to dress him, the process is the same. Instead of the usual way of getting the sleeve ready and taking your baby's arm and putting it in, you invite your baby to become part of the partnership:

We are going to put this top on now - holding up the top for him to see.
Would you give me your hand? - gently touch his hand as a cue for him.
Would you like to give me your hand?
Here, I'll take your hand and put it in the sleeve
Now the other hand? That's the one. - touching his other hand softly.

After a few seconds you take his hand and place the sleeve over it. It will not be many months before your baby will offer you his hand.

Practice makes perfect

To start with you might feel strange talking to your newborn, telling them all that is about to happen. It only seems strange to us because adults don't usually talk to babies in this way, yet this is one of the basic tools which gets your partnership dance off to the very best start.

It was a video of a four-month-old baby girl being changed that set me to finding out about the Pikler Institute in the first place. In the video-clip the parent held up a nappy for the baby to see and said, *"I am going to put a new nappy on, will you lift?"* I thought to myself, *"Yeah right, as if!"* In my eyes, the baby was much too young, but then to my astonishment, the baby lifted her little legs and bottom for her new nappy. In that moment I realised that all I knew about babies was up for very serious revision. I had obviously entirely missed who these amazing Beings really are. So be prepared to be surprised at how early your baby will understand what you are saying and respond to your cues.

Always *with* your baby and never *to* your baby
A baby who is told all that is about to happen before it happens, and who is invited to take part, is one very lucky baby. Her parents have set it up as a respectful partnership from the word go. They respect that she needs to know what is going to happen so that she can feel safe. They do things *with* their baby and not *to* her. There is a critical difference. Although not intended, doing things *to* a baby is the beginning of the abuse of power. It also lays down *the baby's* parenting style.

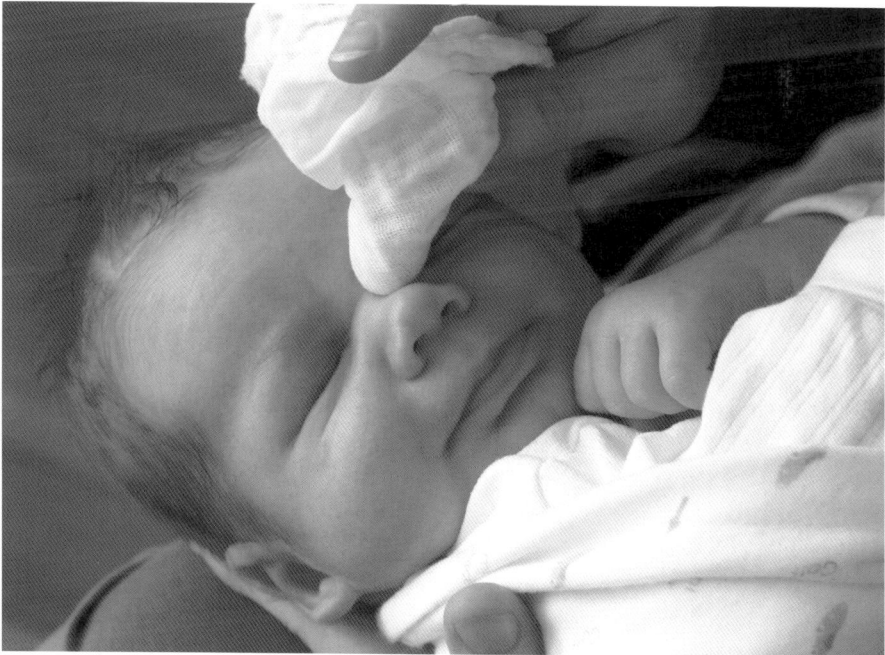

Your new baby is learning to parent

You and I learnt our parenting by hypnosis. Your baby is doing exactly the same when you care for him because his brain operates in the frequency range used in hypnosis. In the first two years his brain operates at the very low frequencies called delta. His brain will operate at theta as well as delta for the next four years until he is six. Delta and theta are pure download states, they are the states for hypnotism. And they are fast. According to Bruce Lipton, your new baby is downloading **everything** *that is going on around him* at four billion bits per second. These downloads form programs in his subconscious which will run his future. Scary stuff, and that is why it makes sense to be loving and respectful when we handle our babies and our children.

How many dancing partners is too many?

In those first days and months your baby doesn't need too many 'dancing partners'. If you were learning a totally new dance from scratch you would probably want to stay with the same partner until you got the hang of the steps. It is the same for your baby, only more so. You are 'home' for your baby, you are the 'known'. From the safety of your heart space your baby has to learn just what these strange large creatures called people are - each person with its own smell, its own sound, its own look, its own frequencies and electromagnetic field. That's a lot to take in, a lot to make sense of. It is very easy for your baby to get into 'sense-ory' overload if you aren't careful, especially in those first days and months. Think about how you would like if you had new people, new experiences, new places coming at you one after the other without a break. And you already *know* about people - your baby is just learning what these strange large creatures are.

Pass the parcel

You have probably noticed already that almost everyone who meets you with your new baby will want to hold her. It is something we do in our culture without thinking - we play 'pass the parcel' with babies. This is doing things *to* babies and not *with* babies. When Emmi Pikler's colleague Magda Gerber was asked if she would like to hold a baby she did not know, she answered famously, *"Does the baby want to be held by me?"* With that one sentence Magda let us know that she had different stories about children from the common ones. Her answer acknowledged that the baby is a free and equal human being, one whose feelings and preferences are to be considered. Her answer acknowledged that the infant-adult partnership is just that: it is a partnership and it is two-way.

Big Day Out with giants
Every day out for a baby is like a Big Day Out, there is so much going on. Remember, you are there to grant your baby his wish to feel safe. That includes safe from sensory overload, and so you can politely turn down baby-holding requests by saying something like, *"That's very kind of you but he has met enough new people today".* They might look at you funny but they'll get over it. You might even give them cause to think about it from a baby's point of view, and if you do, good work. Considering the baby's point of view is one of the ways things are going to get better for babies in this country.

Just imagine that due to some cosmic quirk you landed at the Big Day Out and every single person there was a giant while you were your natural size. What if those big strangers picked you up and started passing you around, *"Oh look at this cute little one, neat eh. Do you wanna have a hold?"* It's my guess you wouldn't feel very safe or calm, and that this wouldn't be your preferred way of meeting people.

A touch of respect

In touch baby
The baby - when he or she arrives - is most vulnerable because, as we have already noted, the baby is still 'foetal' for the first nine months of life outside the womb, the period of *exterogestation*. The baby's skin is a most sensitive organ, constantly taking in and processing information across its whole surface. It is one of the baby's major ways of learning about this new environment outside the womb, and that means Mum. As far as the baby is concerned, Mum is the environment, and it takes almost a year for the baby to 'separate out' and realise Mum is Mum, and I am *me*.

It can be touchy
The quality of touch that the baby receives from us then, is vital, literally. At the Pikler Institute they take great care teaching the nurses how to pick up and hold a baby so that the baby never feels unsupported at any time, in any part of his body. Put yourself in the baby's place: if you are supported (as you were in the womb-water for nine months), you don't have to tense up, you don't have to panic, and you don't have to quickly fire into play muscles that aren't ready for that work yet. You are also learning trust because your 'environment' is trustworthy. The goal of the mother (caregiver) is to handle her baby in such a way that the baby does not have to tense up.

Out of touch
When a baby is tensed or crying she cannot receive the feedback from her own body. We even acknowledge this unconsciously in our language, we say the baby is 'beside herself'. She is 'not there' so to speak. And when a baby is beside herself at the Pikler Institute, they wait. They place a small baby on her back, they stay calm themselves, they put a gentle hand over the baby's heart area with the other hand cradling her head, and they speak tenderly to the distressed child. They would never think of doing anything to the distressed baby, such as changing or dressing her, when she is 'not there'. Just as we would hope that if we ever really lost it in panic in a hospital situation, or at the dentist's, they would wait for us to 'come back to centre' before they did what they had to do.

Soft touch

Handling your baby gently and with confidence cements the First Relationship. If babies are handled like this, they can stay in relationship with themselves. They can receive and process the feedback from their own bodies, because they are not in sensory overload or stress. They are present to, and can respond to their own 'nature', that is, they can respond to their own deepest inner stirrings. It's not rocket science, but if the baby can be in relationship with himself and his own nature, then he is in a very good position to be in relationship with his mother and with her nature and deepest inner stirrings. Ultimately he is in the position to be in relationship with Mother Nature herself, and her deepest inner stirrings, because all babies are designed to do just that. It is this tenderness of touch in the First Relationship that allows the baby the space to have an inner life, to develop an understanding of his own nature, and develop his ability to access the resources that sit within him.

Light touch

Based on his personal enlightenment experience of unbounded joy and happiness, after a very dark night of the soul, Eckhart Tolle in his book *The Power of Now*, speaks to adults who, while worrying about the rates, assignments, climate change and other important things, have lost the key to heaven here on earth. He writes:

"The key is to be in a state of permanent connectedness with your inner body - to feel it at all times. This will rapidly deepen and transform your life. The more consciousness you direct into the inner body, the higher its vibrational frequency becomes. If you keep your attention in the body as much as possible, you will be anchored in the Now. You won't lose yourself in the external world, and you won't lose yourself in your mind. The art of inner-body awareness will develop into a completely new way of living, a state of permanent connectedness with Being, and will add a depth to your life that you have never known before."

Stay in touch

But we have known it before, if only briefly. We were born in touch with our inner-body and with the capacity to stay in touch, and to develop that sensitivity. The gift of tender, gentle, confident touch allows our babies to retain the treasure-inherent that they come with, the treasure that helps them be in relationship.

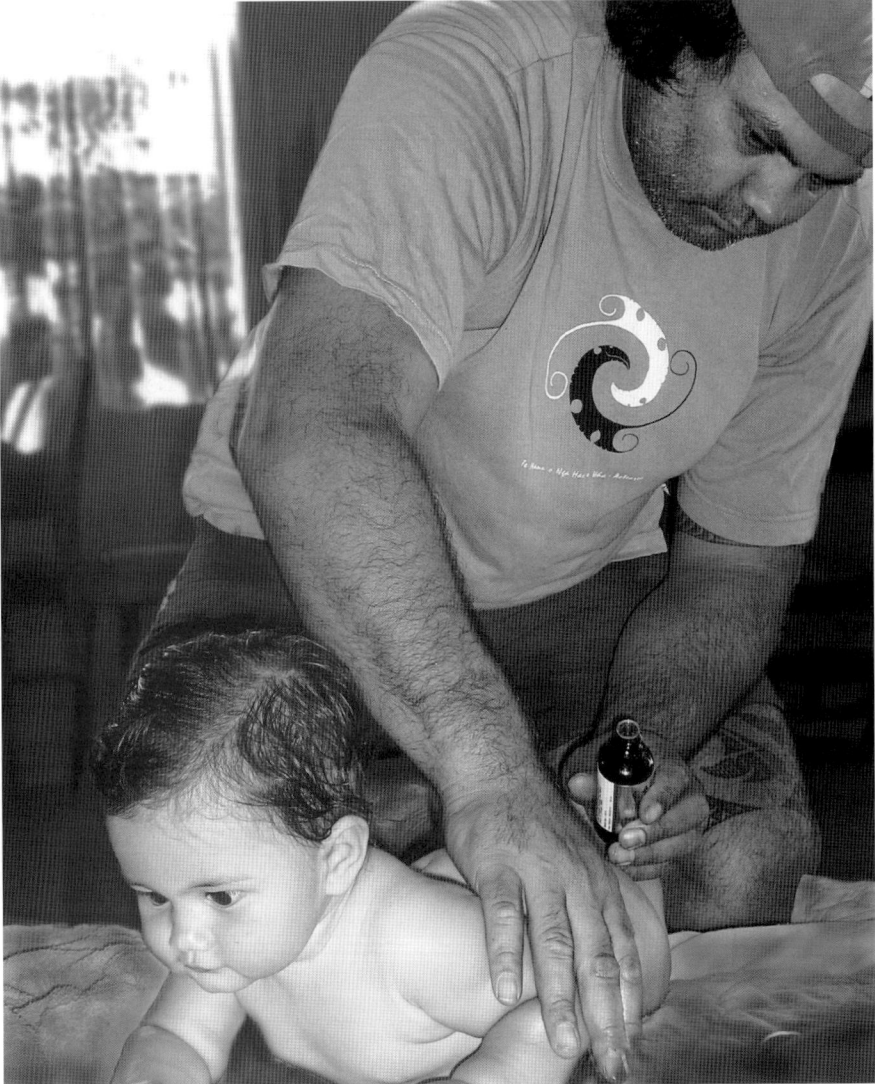

The care moments

The most important moments in your baby's life are not moments with strangers, they are moments spent with you. They are the moments we commonly term 'routines' but that is not a useful name for them because of the way your subconscious interprets the word routine. If you haven't thought about it, the word routine can flick you onto 'automatic pilot'. There, like an automaton, you go through well-known motions but your mind is not there, you are somewhere else. That's okay if you are washing the dishes - though some would disagree - but it's not okay when you are washing a baby. Feeding a baby, dressing her, or changing her with your mind elsewhere means you are not in relationship. Even though you don't intend it, you are treating your baby as a thing and not as a partner.

Full attention

Imagine you were in hospital feeling poorly. If you were bathed and dressed by a nurse who was having a conversation with another in the room, how would you feel? Or if the nurse was lost in his or her own thoughts and ignoring you, it's my guess you would not feel nurtured or understood. You would be more likely to feel like a thing than a person, and you would be nowhere near heart coherence unless you are already a saint.

It's the same when you are talking to someone whose attention is elsewhere, his mind is obviously in another place, he is not with you. At those times you know very clearly that you are not in relationship. You know that there is no partnership because your 'partner' is not there. That is also how it is for the baby. Changing your baby with your mind elsewhere, feeding your baby while you are planning the next day … there are all sorts of ways of being absent, and at the deepest level your baby knows it. Your baby cannot build the partnership with you because you are 'not there'. Older children deal with this very elegantly though: they put their hands either side of your face and turn your head so that you have to make eye contact with them. They know full attention is the key to relating.

Full attention grants wishes

Paying full attention is one of the greatest skills that you can practise in any relationship. It is the gift of yourself to the Other in the interests of love and understanding. Starting on day one there are skills you can use to establish full attention in your partnership with your new baby. Begin with eye contact. Yes, look into your baby's eyes so that she sees your presence. Gently touch her so that she feels your presence. Speak your baby's name - it lets her know that you are there and that something is about to happen. The other great bonus of talking with your baby about every little thing as it is about to happen, is that this practice is full attention in action. It keeps you in the present moment with your child.

It's never routine

Bathing, dressing, feeding and changing are very intimate acts, and they have to be done. You can skip housework with a new baby but you can't skip any of these. Emmi Pikler understood the importance of names and stories, so rather than calling these activities routines, she called them 'care moments'. She knew, and taught, that they are the most important moments in the whole of your baby's life. Done with respect and full attention, these are the moments which make and cement the relationship. She taught her nurses that the relationship is *all*, it is a matter of life to the baby. What happens in the care moments decides the quality of the relationship and, if you think about it, that's just common sense. Of course if people treat you 'respect-full-y', if they are gentle and careful with you, if they delight in your company and your input, then your partnership cannot help but flourish.

Bonus bonds

There's another bonus when you pay full attention during the care moments aside from the relationship bonds that it makes. When you pay full attention to your baby in the care moments it fills your baby's 'emotional tanks'. When she isn't running on 'emotional empty' she is able to have time by herself without needing you. Magda Gerber termed this 'wants nothing time'. Emotionally satiated, your baby can put all of her being into play and exploration, right from the earliest days. The parents who treat their babies like this tell me that this was an unexpected, yet much appreciated bonus. And all as a result of paying full attention.

Full attention is...
Full attention is the key to great partnerships - you could say it is love in action. Certainly, when you see it practised, it looks like it. More importantly, it *feels* like it and that is one of the three wishes, to feel loved. Eckhart Tolle goes further: *"Wisdom is not the product of thought. The deep knowing that is wisdom arises through the simple act of giving something or someone your full attention. Attention is primordial intelligence, consciousness itself.... It joins the perceiver and the perceived in a unifying field of awareness. It is the healer of separation."*
This is his way of saying that full attention brings people into heart coherence, into partnership, and much more.

Baby genius

Getting into everything

As Eckhart Tolle says, the deep knowing that is wisdom arises from the simple act of paying something (or someone) your full attention. You have seen your baby doing this, totally engrossed with something, soaking it all in like a sponge, through his senses. Babies are designed to do this. They have two major 'programs' running in their first four years, programs which open and start operating at birth: the first is to bond with Mum and stay bonded with her because she is, as we noted earlier, the known. The second program is to explore the world - the unknown - with everything they have got. That means getting into everything. You have probably noticed that too.

Are you an ally or adversary?

This is where your baby needs you as an ally and not as an obstacle.

That doesn't mean that your baby should wreck the place, of course he shouldn't. It does mean that you need to know what your baby needs so that you can be his learning ally. A learning ally knows just how to set it up so that babies can learn 'to their heart's content'. A baby in heart coherence is a pure learning machine.

Your baby is a genius - in potential
If you, like many others, still hold to the old story that intelligence is a fixed quotient, then it's time for an update for your baby's sake. Intelligences are not fixed, some people do not get 'heaps of brains' while others miss out. All of the intelligences are in every baby as potentials, and they grow and develop according to the models and the experiences available to the child. The baby needs to be in the presence of someone - the model - who has developed that intelligence themselves. That way the baby has the experiences which are part of that intelligence, and paradoxically, these experiences develop the intelligence in the baby at the same time.

You are the model
For example: (hearing) babies are capable of speaking any of the more than 6,000 languages spoken on this planet. The potential is there to speak any language, or many languages. It will all depend on the model as to how much of that potential is made real, or 'real-ised'. Models 'open the files' in the baby's brain, and like computer files, once a file is opened it can be added to at any time. My daughter had me as her model so she is monolingual and she speaks New Zealand English with a Thames accent. Had she had a bilingual parent who spoke to her in both languages she would have realised much more of her potential, She would have made many more connections in the 'language file' in her brain, and she would find languages much easier to learn than she does. Still, her language file *was* opened and she can add to it any time she wants to. The 'files' do have to be opened for the intelligence to begin to be realised. Some files are very time specific, if they are not opened by their 'open by date' they are deleted, boom, gone.

Your brainy baby

Brain researchers tell us that every baby comes with around one hundred billion brain cells. That's a number too hard to imagine for most of us, so scientists liken it to the number of stars in the Milky Way galaxy. That's still pretty hard to imagine, but you get the idea; that it is a *lot* of potential. It really is phenomenal how much potential Nature has gifted your baby. At birth only about 15% of those brain cells are wired up. The other 85% of brain cells need to be 'wired up', the neurons need to make their connections.

In the mood for learning

With all of that potential waiting to be unfolded, your baby needs to be in the right mood - or the right emotional state - so that he can get on with physically 'wiring up his brain'. You will remember that paying full attention fills your baby's 'emotional tanks'. When a baby is emotionally full he is in the perfect emotional state for learning. It is your caring and nurturing that frees him to develop his other great talent, learning to learn.

A body of knowledge

Put a different way: because the deepest part of your baby's being is not emotionally needy he can get on with learning with *all* of his being. Your emotionally satisfied baby takes learning very seriously and gives it 100% of his attention, for surprisingly long periods of time. It is your care which frees him to develop a 'body of learning', learning with his body, and at the same time wiring up his brain.

Dance and play

Learning is a dance too

Being able to move the body is imperative for the dance of learning. All babies learn to move and move to learn, the two are one and the same. When someone has had a stroke and part of the brain is affected, there is a corresponding effect in the body. Body and brain are part of the same unit; they affect each other, and the learning dance requires that babies *move*.

Learning to move is moving to learn

The choreography for The Dance of Life is exactly the same wisdom which grew the baby in the womb. That wisdom doesn't stop just because the baby is born. Of course it keeps expressing itself, but now that the baby is born it needs our support so that it can continue to express itself as designed. Dr Pikler spent thousands of hours observing thousands of babies. She wanted to learn how babies moved if they were allowed to follow their inbuilt moving-choreography, naturally, without help or interference.

Supporting the dance

You and I wouldn't buy a young specimen tree from a nursery, plant and stake it, then place a garden seat over the top of it. We wouldn't place the seat over the tree because we'd know that the tree wouldn't be able to follow its choreography and grow towards the heavens. This is an absurd example of us getting in the way of the Dance of Life. In less obvious ways we do this to babies, particularly during that important first year of their dance.

Free human beings are free to move

While we all agree that of course babies are free and equal human beings, we do employ a lot of devices to stop them moving *in the way their development requires*: safe sleeping devices, highchairs, baby swings, various 'jolly-activity-walker-exerciser-bouncing-jumping' containers, bath chairs... the list goes on and on. If we haven't thought about it too deeply, we might think that these devices are for the baby's safety, or we may have bought into the manufacturer's spiel that these devices are educational. They do not develop your baby's intelligences as claimed, and with the exception of the car seat in the moving car and the cot, these devices are not for safety either. They are for adult convenience. There would be nothing wrong with that if they were good for the baby as well, but they aren't.

Containers are for ships, not baby geniuses

The baby's body is driven to respond to inner choreography by moving at least once every 30 seconds. Instead, some babies are spending up to 30 waking hours a week in restraining containers, devices in which it is not

possible to do what is required to unfold genius. Use your imagination and put yourself in the baby's place. If you were strapped into any restraining container for long periods of time you would probably call it torture and sue the perpetrator.

Baby gym

It helps parents when they are thinking about infant workouts to liken them to their own workouts in the gym. If, instead of you working out, your trainer 'got kind' and did the exercises that you yourself needed for your strength and fitness, that wouldn't be of any use to you. Kind though it seems, you wouldn't make any progress. Same with your baby. We adults too often get in there and do things for babies and deprive them of the pleasure of the workout, and for babies, workouts are pure pleasure. We are in so much of a hurry, we tummy them, sit them, stand them and walk them long before they could get there for themselves. Dr Pikler realised from her thousands of hours of observations that the last thing babies need is to be put into positions that they can't get into or out of by themselves. That is us doing things *to* the baby. That's us taking away from the baby the chance to work out and develop balance, muscles, strength, and all in the fine-tuned choreographic sequence which leads to perfect posture.

Lucky baby

Very lucky is the baby whose parents know that their baby will work out and make all of these milestones by themselves, unassisted. Not only does that baby have a better opportunity to unfold much more of the potential of his physical intelligence, he also gets to develop more useful qualities of character. These babies learn about effort, stickability, frustration, more effort, and success. The pure joy of the baby when he has achieved a milestone in his dance is like the buzz you and I get when we expend a lot of effort and achieve a goal. It would definitely not feel half as good if someone did it for us.

Save money

You probably already have all that you need for an ideally equipped baby gym because you have a floor. When new babies want to work out all they need is a good firm flat surface under them. A firm flat mattress in the cot is their first gym equipment, and later they will want to graduate to the floor. Babies need to lie on their backs during their workouts. On the back they can exercise their arms and legs, their neck muscles by rolling their head from one side to the other, and most importantly, they can develop their inner core strength by flexing their wee bodies this way and that.

Infant Pilates

Working out on the back, your baby will eventually get to turn onto one side, then the other side. She will spend many weeks balancing and playing on her back and her sides, fine tuning her core strength and her balance as she works out different sets of muscles. My friend Luke, a professional exponent of modern dance, tells me that core strength is the key to dance. So although it can *appear* that nothing much is happening for your baby, the ground work is being laid. Resist the temptation to interfere and assist.

Hold off and trust because suddenly one day, when her muscles have developed enough balance and strength, your baby will turn onto her tummy. You and I don't have to help with any of this development, we just need to ensure that she gets the time to work out uninterrupted. Remember, this choreography is *in* your baby, it is in every baby. You need to understand the dance so you can support your baby's unfolding.

Tummy time - take one
In New Zealand you might well be advised to put your baby onto her tummy before she can do that for herself. Dr Pikler, in her more than 60 years of experience with all those babies, discovered that babies who are allowed to work out and follow their inbuilt choreography have no need to be put onto their tummies. Her research uncovered no advantages, though it did show up that babies who had had tummy time were statistically more likely to fall when walking. If you want to do tummy time, the kind that does have myriads of advantages is the age old practice of putting your baby onto *your* tummy. That way the two of you are lying there heart to heart, relaxed, in heart coherence, in love.

Tummy time - take two

Now that your baby has had enough workout time to get *herself* onto
her tummy she will begin the tummy workouts and this is very hard work
because she has to hold up her heavy head. Fortunately she has already
spent a lot of time on her back, rolling her head from side to side. The toys
you placed either side of her encouraged her to work out her neck muscles.
There was no weight on those muscles, but she was preparing them for
the day when she would make it to her tummy. Now that she is there,
she is on her way along - along the floor. She'll work out until she can roll
along, creep along, slither along, along-sideways, along-backwards, along-
frontwards, and eventually crawl along. Along the way she will develop
extraordinary flexibility, balance, and strength, not to mention how much of
the potential intelligences in her body and brain will be wired up. All of these
benefits - and more - are achieved just by allowing your baby to follow her
inbuilt choreography.

Back to front and front to back

Those early stages of moving from back to front, and front to back again
can be very challenging. When your baby finally gets to his tummy he will
experience frustration because for the first week or so his arm will almost
always be stuck underneath him. Neither is he able to get 'home' again
onto his back. These are crucial stages in your baby's learning to learn,
so get down there with him and support him, reading his cues. When the
frustration builds you acknowledge his communication, *"You got yourself
onto your tummy but now your arm is stuck, I can see it's frustrating."* You
don't rescue him first up, you allow your baby time to problem solve with your
support. *"You did get your arm out, good going."* And when it is too much, *"I
see this is too much frustration for now, I will place you back onto your back."*
When you allow and support your baby to solve the problems of moving his
own body, a part of his body of knowledge will be as a problem solver.

Sitting follows crawling

As soon as she can get to her knees she is on her way to sitting. The babies
who are lucky enough never to have been propped in the sitting position

always sit *after* they get to their knees. At first it's a kind of half-sit using an arm for balance. When they do sit unsupported, they sit as though they were yoga instructors so perfect is their posture. They *never* fall over and hit their heads, and they can get out of sitting as quickly as they got into it. Contrast that with the poor baby who is plonked into the sitting position. She has to be propped so she won't fall and crack her precious head with that sickening thud. She cannot follow the promptings within which tell her to go and explore. She cannot move. She is in an invisible container. Eventually - weeks or months later - she will find a way to obey the dance choreography and she will bum-shuffle to the object which is calling out to be explored. Good on her for being resourceful enough to find a way around it, but contrast the pleasure, growth and development she has, or doesn't have, to the baby who is free to move through the 'along workout'.

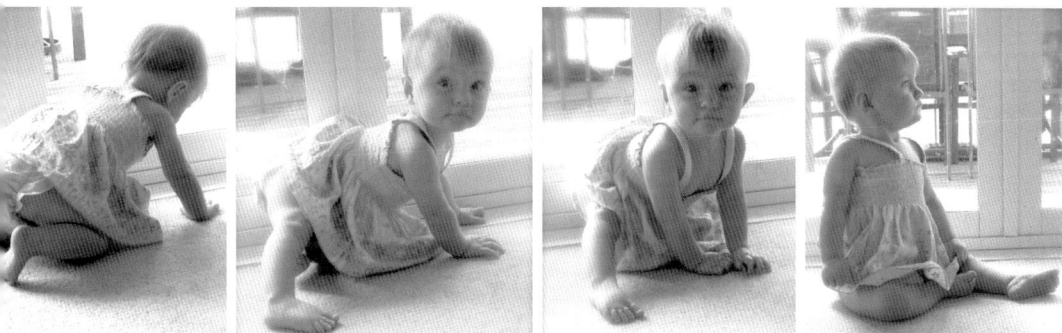

Moving along

What your baby needs is equipment that will support the back work out, the side work out, the tummy work out, the getting-up-onto-things work out, and the up and running work out. Until your baby is on his tummy and getting up onto things, the floor is all you need. When babies want to creep and slither onto things, the firm cushions off your couch are perfect. They learn to climb up on them and to climb down. They also learn to fall off them. Falling without injury is a great skill to learn, and babies learn it with ease from a height where they cannot do themselves any damage. You can borrow equipment specially designed by Emmi Pikler (and made here in New Zealand by Starex) from better toy libraries. These simple pieces extend baby workouts safely, but your baby can do all she needs to do on the floor and the furniture.

If it's not broken don't fix it
Around our country parent-initiated baby-movement activities are being promoted; activities such as putting a baby on a skate board and moving him along, or holding him with his head lower than his feet and gently moving the him with a circular motion. These activities have been developed as a result of research into why young children are failing at school. It turns out, not surprisingly, that as babies these failing scholars didn't get to do the workouts their bodies had to have to allow their potential genius to unfold. The response to the research is a set of special activities designed to ensure that babies do develop what they will need later on. All well and good, except there is the built-in assumption that your baby won't get to work out, and therefore she will need these 'remedial' activities. If your baby has time on the floor to work out in her waking hours there will be no need for you to interfere and do things *to* her. She will follow her inbuilt choreography and be 'all systems go', naturally. That's the way Nature designed her.

Flat head fears
There is also a fear out there that if babies spend all their time on their backs the back of their heads will flatten out. One American professional website carries photos of babies with flat heads, enough to put the fear into any parent. Many of the containers used with young babies keep their heads stuck in same position with the pressure unrelieved. Even plush sheepskins or mats can do the same. The baby settles down into a comfy nest and cannot move her head from side to side to relieve pressure. So in those first months if all of baby's sleeping hours and waking hours put unrelieved pressure onto the back of the head a flat head can result. If, however, your baby has a firm flat mattress and the floor to work out on during her waking hours she will have a perfectly normal head.

Play and grow

Scientists need equipment

There's no need to go shopping to get toys to develop your child's intelligences despite what the advertising brochures tell you. Sure, 'baby-bling' keeps retailers happy, but with a bit of thought you can save your money and save the planet from disappearing under mountains of plastic. Give your baby a better start by being imaginative and resourceful. The very first 'toys' your little scientist will want to spend lots of time playing with won't cost you a thing, they are on the end of his arms: his hands. Firstly, he has to discover that he *has* hands and next that they are a part of *him*.

Finger play

His hands come with a clutch reflex, which means his hands are clenched. This reflex has to fade away for his fingers to straighten out. We can unwittingly delay this by giving tiny babies things to hold all the time. I know there is nothing lovelier for us than to have a tiny baby clutch a finger, but let's not go putting toys in their hands thereby slowing things down. When the clutch reflex has gone, a baby who has some time on his own without anyone waving things in front of his face and putting things in his hands will do what babies have always done since the beginnings of time - he will play with his hands. This will be one of his favourite games for his first three months and it is an important game. The more practice he gets, the better his dexterity. He is getting his 'equipment' ready so that when he *can* move around he will have just the right skills to pick up what he sees and explore it.

Something to play with

Your baby wants to explore everything because *everything* is new and interesting for her. Her powerful learning drive dictates that she must get hold of every interesting thing and put it in her mouth. That way she will soak in the most information to build up her body of knowledge. That's why those baby-frames adults hang over babies aren't great for babies. The frustrated baby is perpetually playing piggy-in-the-middle because she can't action her learning programme; she can't get those things and put them in her mouth. Some really flash versions of those frames are a

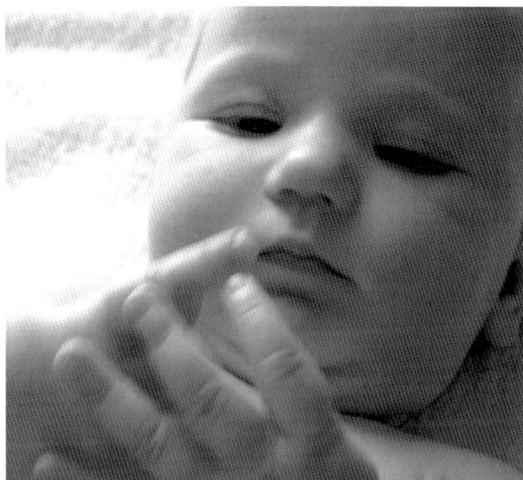

sensory-overload nightmare for any baby new to this world. Babies senses aren't jaded, babies are not seeking more and more novelty in the way teens and adults do. *Everything* is new and novel for them.

Take your pick

Since this early wiring-up is the foundation for all that will follow, it is worth putting some thought into what you choose. You are granting her wish to be safe, so you pick what she will play with. You are keeping her safe from sensory overload, from swallowing things, and from injuring herself. You are also picking things which will fascinate her, things which will allow her to learn the laws of this three dimensional physical reality, things which will open her intelligences to nature and to beauty.

Back play

Choosing toys for a young baby on his back needs special consideration. The baby will be learning to make his hands work the way he wants them to, so choose things which are really easy for him to hold onto. He will be holding the toy above his face it so it needs to be light. That way it doesn't take too much energy to play with it for long periods, and if he drops it, it isn't going to hurt him.

Love and play

Next to being loved and nurtured, play is the most important thing in the baby's world. Play is the generic intelligence, it is the activity which opens the files of all the other intelligences. Play for your baby means being free to move in her body because moving is playing for a baby. Play also means being free to choose what to play with (from the selection you provide), and being free to play with it for as little or as long as she wants. Then there is the play that you do together, this is the loving play that lays their foundations for their lifetime of playing with others. This play includes singing lullabies, songs and jingles, dancing around the kitchen with your baby-partner in your arms, making funny faces and just generally hanging out.

Tickling is not funny

But keep it gentle in those early months. Babies need a slow and gentle introduction to the world of play, one that doesn't put their little systems into overload. Some people think that tickling is something babies like. They don't, but they can't tell you that. Most of us remember being tickled when we were children and we remember how horrible it was. Even though we were laughing we didn't think it was funny, but the tickling adult would not stop. Tickling is not about respect, it is a misreading of the babies' cues. Bouncing babies and hoisting them high in the air is not respectful either. Leave the rough-and-tumble play until much later. Wait till they are older toddlers, then if they ask you for more excitement you will know that it is their choice, they are ready for it. You will still need to read their cues to see when enough is enough though.

A word of respect

Journey to independence

The journey for babies is a journey to independence. That means learning to use and to trust their own judgement; it means learning to follow the curiosity that arises from within. Babies and children need to experience the satisfaction that comes from achieving their goals. That satisfaction itself is their reward for their effort. It becomes their motivation. This journey to

independence is either encouraged or smothered by the way we behave and speak with our children.

Out with the old, in with the new
Earlier we looked at how talking with your baby helps get your partnership dance off to a brilliant start. When you give your child notice of everything that is about to happen, every time, it soon becomes your new habit. But some of the old habits that we have caught around speaking to children undermine the very things we want for our children. If we stop and hear what we are saying, we will probably want to fine-tune things a bit.

Sweet talk
Some of us grew up on a bit of a starvation diet in the encouragement department. Feeling that a bit more acknowledgement would have been welcome for us, we endeavour to do that for our children. We want to encourage and acknowledge them. It is a basic human need to be noticed. In Africa, a Zulu greeting translates as *I see you. Oh yes, I see you.* So how

do we tell our children we 'see them' in a way that encourages them on their journey to independence as well as in their self esteem?

Habits of speech

Nearly all of the things we say to babies and children are habits of speech for us. In our culture it has been a habit to comment on the *child* - who he is, and not the *action* - what he does. That probably means that is what you do, you will have caught our culture's habit. Making ascriptive statements - commenting on who the child is - can have some serious side effects. For the negative statements it can seem pretty obvious:

> *You are a liar. You are a grizzler.*
> *You can't share can you? You are so naughty.*
> *You are such a pig with your food. You are a bad boy.*
> *By golly, you are disobedient.*

Sticky labels

This is labelling or name calling. Each label is really a mini-story, and we have already looked at how very powerful stories are. The Navajo have a saying: *"The sacred begins at the tip of the tongue. Be careful when speaking. You create the world around you with your words."* Who in their right mind would want any baby to take on the following labels as their defining story from which to create their lives?

You are such a naughty little boy.
Go to sleep you naughty girl.
You idiot, you never listen.
Fiddle fingers, I told you not to touch that.
Oh stop it. You are just a cry baby.

Am I a Divine Child?

A baby is forming his image of who he is in this world. Children don't come with a self image; their self image grows from the way they are handled and spoken to. These negative statements are not respectful and they are not partnership. They build the exact image that parents don't want because children who 'know' they are grizzly and naughty will *be* grizzly and naughty. They have very little choice because of the way that language works.

As Deepak Chopra says:
"Telling a child what he is makes a much deeper impression than telling him what to do. The mind-body system actually organises itself around such verbal experiences, and the wounds delivered in words can create far more permanent effects than physical trauma, for literally we create ourselves out of words."
Sticks and stones may break my bones - but names can be even more dangerous!

Describe acknowledge describe
So instead of insulting our babies and toddlers, we need to develop the habit of describing. Describing helps your baby make more sense of the world and does not leave him feeling shamed and wrong. Your baby or toddler will still feel safe, loved and respected when you describe.

Check out these examples of changing name calling - the sentence in grey - into respectful language.

You idiot, you are so clumsy.
Whoops, everywhere. We'll wipe it up.
You are a grizzler.
Sounds to me like you could be tired.
You are a naughty boy.
Your toys go in the box, pop them in please.
You are such a pig with your food.
Use your spoon for your yoghurt.
You can't share can you?
Xena is playing with that. That's hers for now.
You are a liar.
Saying you did it isn't easy sometimes.
You are so disobedient.
I asked you to leave it for your sister to eat.

You are such a cry baby
You are very upset. That's really made you unhappy.

Respect feelings

Describing like this is respectful. It acknowledges what has happened, what needs to happen, and it does it in a way that the baby - and the speaker - can stay in touch with their hearts. When babies are upset they know instinctively how to let that emotional energy work itself out. They are brilliant at letting it all out, and then coming back into coherence - if we let them. All we have to do is acknowledge what is going on for them. Describing does that. If, however, you put the lid on their emotions by shaming them, they learn that how *they* deal with emotions is not acceptable to *you*. They learn that feelings are too dangerous to deal with, so they let that emerging skill die in order to stay in your 'good books'. The price we pay for this is way too dear. These babies lose their real, true selves just to please you. They grow into adults with little or no emotional intelligence, and emotional intelligence is one of the key ingredients in making successful intimate relationships.

More sticky labels

Making ascriptive statements that are positive is not as damaging as for negative statements, but they can have negative side effects too. It's just that they aren't so obvious at first glance.

You are such a good girl. You are really clever.
You're my favourite helper.

The little person hearing these statements can easily become addicted to what others think of her and end up seeking approval for all that she does. She can even end up believing that her worth depends upon others' opinions of her, which, of course, it doesn't. Looking to the outside for approval interferes with her experiencing reward and inner satisfaction when she has chosen and completed a task on her journey to independence. And that's where the value of talking about what the child *does* comes in.

Describe and acknowledge

When you comment on what the child *does*, the child still feels seen. The deep human need for attention is met. The verbal acknowledgement of the achievement or task helps the child to appreciate exactly what it is that they have achieved. It gives them the words to describe what they have achieved and it also signals what is expected behaviour around your place.

You are such a good girl.
Thanks, you put that where Baby could reach.
You are really clever.
You pulled yourself up, good going.
You're my favourite helper.
I really appreciated your help putting the toys away.
You are a genius.
You did the puzzle all by yourself. It was a tricky one too.
Oh good boy.
You are so gentle with Moose, he likes you patting him.

Changing habits

For most of us, having satisfying relationships with little people (and big people) means we have to ditch some of the patterns of speaking we picked up along the way. Learning to describe and acknowledge what is happening without judging follows on easily from your new habit of telling your baby everything that is about to happen before it happens, because that too is describing. The time you take to learn the habit of acknowledging without judgement will be one of the biggest investments you can make in your baby's future as a happy, well-adjusted human being. It will also make the job of parenting so much easier and enjoyable when your baby reaches toddlerhood. That's worth going for.

Baby Sign Language - take one

People often ask me what I think about Baby Sign Language: speaking with your baby in the sign language which she learns from you. Baby Sign Language lets you know what is going on for your baby, and it lets her know what you want. It has to be good. It is another language. It makes more connections in the baby's language file, and in yours. I believe the real value of baby signing is that it makes you the parent pay full attention to your baby. You *have* to be facing each other, paying full attention and observing your baby when you are speaking and listening in sign.

Baby sign language - take two

Your baby is born 'signing'. She speaks the universal baby language of vowels, each with its own meaning, and she gives you very clear signs right from the word go. Instead of expecting your baby to learn from you, you could reverse it and learn from your baby. If you pay full attention, observe and practise the respectful conduct outlined in this book you will quickly learn a richer, more subtle baby sign language, this time on your baby's terms. It is really up to you to decide whether you want to go with what you and your baby already have in place and develop that, or if you want to learn another language to pass it on.

Start the way you want it to continue

Independent or helpless?

For some funny reason, our culture seems to think that there is a time of 'being a baby', in which you treat babies as helpless, and then there is a time when the baby 'turns into a child'. At that time you switch what you have been doing and you treat the child differently because you want him or her to become independent.

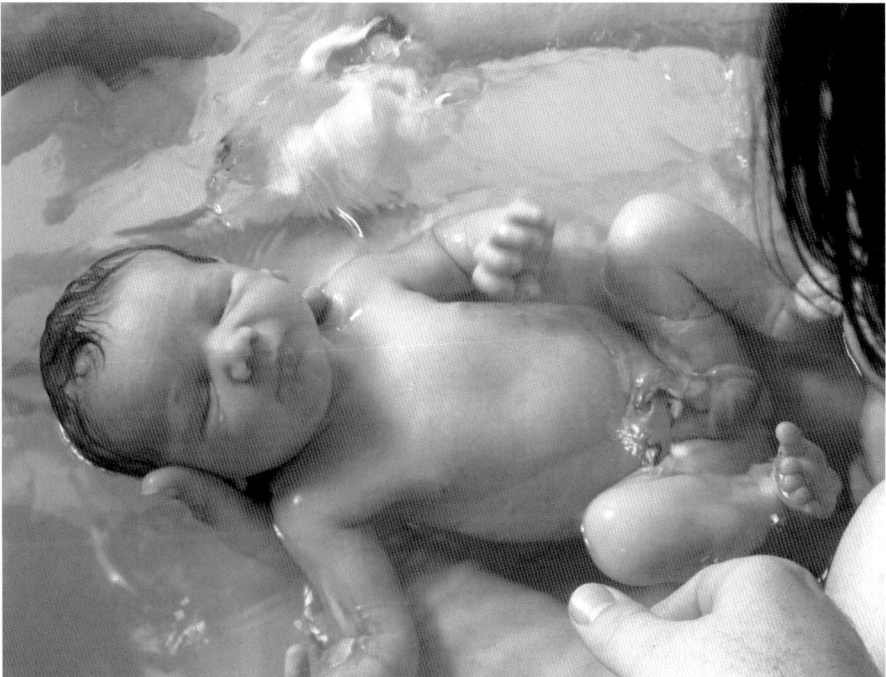

Learned helplessness

Too late! If you treat babies as helpless, before you can say, *"Where's the dummy?"* the babies will have learned helplessness because they are such quick learners. Babies learn how to be helpless, they are not born helpless. As we have noted they are born capable and wise in their own way. If you haven't thought about it, it can be very easy to teach a baby to be helpless instead of capable and independent. Lets look at some of the things that people commonly do, or don't do, probably because they haven't thought through what each one teaches.

Yoo hoo, anybody home?

I recently sat beside a mother with her baby in a pram outside Sky City. The baby was smiling to his mum in a sustained attempt to communicate, but mum's mind was elsewhere. She didn't know about full attention. Who knows, she may have lost a fortune, but she also missed the treasure right before her eyes. And her son? Well he was pretty helpless in his best attempts to relate to the-centre-of-the-universe, his mum. Too much of that and he would not perceive himself as being a powerful and independent being. He would either give up, or he would up the ante and try less charming ways of getting himself noticed, of making his mark in the world. Unless we knew better, we might say that he was naughty and attention seeking.

Let me get it

Many babies are placed under 'entertainment structures' when that is the last thing they need if they are going to unfold their intelligences. Babies are born with an internal program that demands they take hold of anything that looks interesting, and proceed to learn all about it. One of the main ways a baby learns about things is by putting them in her mouth. When you understand that, you can see why hanging toys and objects in your baby's line of sight is helplessness training; she can't get hold of them and she can't put them in her mouth to learn all about them. She is also helpless because she can't get away from them either, and let's face it, some of those things they hang over babies are pretty darn ugly.

Please let me get it

When there is a range of things to play with, let the babies choose what takes their interest. Too many adults choose the play thing when babies are perfectly capable of making the right selections for themselves. When the baby chooses what is interesting to *him*, he is following *his* own internal

promptings, learning what interests him, and how to follow that up. He will play with it until the internal promptings take his interest elsewhere. He is learning that he has the power to make choices in his life, such an important step on the road to independence.

Please let me choose

Don't you hate it when you are watching a program on the television, you are interested in it, then someone grabs the remote and *hey presto,* you are watching something else? When we choose something we are interested in, we like to stay with it until we have lost interest in it. We are not that keen on having someone else inflict their interests onto us. It's the same for a baby. When babies have been allowed to choose what interests them, they need time to explore and play until they are not interested any more.

Grown-ups often 'change channels' on babies by picking up a toy and waving it in front of the baby when she was right in the middle of a 'different program'. This lack of thought and respect teaches the baby that her choices aren't important, and that she does not need to entertain herself, someone will entertain her. A baby who learns to be entertained will want to be entertained. This is what my mother would have called 'making a rod for your own back', because it actively discourages independence, and it stops the baby from growing her attention span.

Why do you want to see me stuck?
Putting babies into any position that they cannot get into or out of by

themselves is helplessness training too. While they have movements they are capable of, they cannot exercise them when they have been put in a position that they cannot achieve for themselves. If we revisit the baby placed on the tummy before she can get there herself, we will see how her independence is swapped for helplessness. This baby can wave her arms, kick her legs, roll her head from side to side, focus and see out of both her eyes. These steps in her dance she does with ease. Put her on her tummy and now she can do none of these, she is stuck. The position is itself an invisible container, and like other containers, it constitutes helplessness training.

What is the hurry?
Propping babies to sit, supporting them to stand, and holding them to walk is more than helplessness training. Physically, it forces babies to use muscles and skeletal structure not yet ready for the task, but emotionally the cost may be even higher. As Magda Gerber so succinctly puts it, *"How must it affect infants when what they **can** do is not appreciated, and what they cannot do is expected?"* Is this the beginning of that all too pervasive story, 'I do not measure up'?

Sooner does not equal smarter
There is no hurry. It's reassuring for you to know that babies who are allowed to unfold to the choreography of their internal body wisdom very often take longer to reach milestones such as sitting and walking. That's because Nature does things properly and doesn't take short cuts. There are no competitions for getting born first, rolling over first, crawling first, or for getting your teeth first. Getting there first doesn't say anything at all about how clever your baby is. Your baby would like you to know this so that you don't succumb to the pressure from others around you who seem to think that getting there sooner equals smarter. Even Albert Einstein's parents reportedly worried because he was so slow to learn to speak. They didn't know that sooner does not equal smarter. Every baby in the world is unique with his or her own unique fingerprints, DNA, iris patterns, voice prints *and* timing. If a genius like Albert Einstein took *his* time learning to speak, you can respect that your baby will unfold her genius in her own good time too.

Going public

Respect my timing

In these hurried days, more and more parents are taking their babies to baby classes, not all of which are beneficial. There are classes which leave your baby (and you) feeling safe, loved and respected, but you need to seek them out. These are parent-infant classes where you will learn at least as much as your baby does by being there. These classes are about the partnership dance and they promote and strengthen your relationship with your baby. There are also baby classes where the focus is on trying to teach the baby something - baby swimming, baby music, baby dance, baby gymnastics. How do you assess whether these classes are beneficial for your baby? Ask yourself these few questions to help you differentiate:

*Will it be **to** the baby?*

Will my baby be expected to do what someone else decides is good for him? Or will my baby be able to choose what he does, how he does it and when he does it?

Am I wanting to rush things?

Am I thinking about baby music when my baby is still delighted when we sing and dance with him, when we clap time and play music with together? Am I thinking about baby-gym when my baby is really happy learning to roll, or learning to crawl on the couch cushions, climb on the couch, or to run up and down the hallway?

Is the class safe from sensory overload?

Is the class noisy with many parents and babies?

Or is the class small, intimate and peaceful with no more than eight parents and their babies?

Do the class leaders model respect for each baby?

Does the class leader greet each baby by name?

Is the class leader unhurried and peaceful? Do they demonstrate knowledge of a baby's development by *allowing* it to unfold?

How embarrassing

When you do take your baby to gatherings with other parents and babies it can be ultra stressful, especially when babies are learning about each other. You may have even taken your baby to baby group where he was very active - active taking toys from the other children. You may have wanted to leave hurriedly, or deliver your baby a crash course in sharing. If you and the other adults don't understand that learning to share takes between two and three years, it can be really embarrassing.

Me and mine

Recall that it will take your baby the whole first year to work out that he is a separate person, separate from you. Only then is he ready to learn that he is a *me*, and an *I*. Once he gets that idea firmly under his belt, he is in a position to start exploring *mine*. A baby who hasn't worked out *me* and *mine* certainly can't manage the concept of sharing. Sharing requires that he advances from *me* and *mine* to become aware of *you* and *yours*. Only when he is aware of *me*, *mine*, *you* and *yours* can he see that *you* might like his. The bad news is that this can take at least two years.

Bullies and victims

In the meantime how do you manage the baby group gatherings in a way that doesn't set children up in the roles of bullies and victims? When an infant takes a toy from another it is not done with malice. A toy on the floor doesn't move, but when it is picked up suddenly it 'comes alive' and becomes much more interesting. The infant who wasn't interested in the toy when it was still goes for the 'alive' toy single-mindedly. The baby is *not* fighting the other child. He is after the toy and picking up a toy from the carpet or taking it from a hand - what's the difference if you haven't worked out *yours* and *mine*?

Be nice, you've got to share

Well, for starters the carpet doesn't get upset that you have taken the toy, so let's deal with the child who has lost the toy first. Observe the child and if she is not upset there is no reason for you to be upset either. If the child *is* upset, you need to acknowledge their feelings because they will be awash with emotion, and you can help them make sense of that. In a calm and centred way comment on what has happened, without any judgement. So you will not say, *"Oh you poor thing, Jason was very naughty taking that from you,"* but *"I can see you are upset, really upset."* That way Jason is not cast into the role of a naughty bully, and the other child doesn't get scripted into the role of victim. These roles can stick if you aren't careful - and you wouldn't want that. It is a terrible start for a child when adults give him destructive self images to internalise unconsciously. You could offer another similar toy, *"Here is another ball. Would you like this one?"* Next time you can also give the child permission to hold on if they want to keep a toy, *"Hold on if you want to keep the toy Hana."*

What about Jason?
If you can get there before he takes the toy, you can offer him a similar toy, *"I can see you want a ball Jason. Here is one you could play with."* If you get there as the tug of war is going on, while you ensure no-one is hurt, you can turn the problem over to them rather than solve it for them. What you won't do is sort it for them. If you take the ball from Jason to give it back to Hana because 'she had it first' you have just 'done a Jason' yourself. How will babies make sense of that when it doesn't make sense? If instead you turn your hands palms up (see pages 81-83) and offer, *"I see you both want the same thing. What can we do?"* toddlers will stop, look at you and most often they will sort it out themselves. Your waiting peaceably, palms up, allows them the time to work through their inner maelstrom of feelings to a peaceable solution.

Gently does it
Children will be as gentle with each other as they have been treated themselves, yet still children pull hair, mouth (bite), and hurt others. Firstly, this *must be stopped straight away*, firmly and gently, but it is important for adults to realise that this hurting is not done with malice. This is the infant learning about this amazing world they have landed in. There is a lot to learn and it takes an infant a long long time to learn that getting handfuls of that interesting stuff called hair hurts and causes another child to cry. We

can help the process of them working out cause and effect by gently telling them, *"When you pull hair it hurts Jason."*

It is enough to put your hand between the child wanting to explore hair and the hair while saying, *"I can't let you pull Jason's hair. It hurts him."*

Be nice, you've got to be patient

Children will share as soon as they have the all the learnings in place that make sharing possible. If you understand what they have to learn and support them while they are doing it, they will get there with elegance. Children supported in this way astound adults with their mature and peaceful play.

Biting

Having practised all of the above with their babies, some parents find that their baby still bites. Within a baby-battling setting both the parent and

baby quickly become the pariahs at the baby classes. *"Bite them back"* is not uncommon advice for bitten babies, *"Go on, bite them back. Hard."* This kind of advice doesn't keep anyone in heart coherence and it certainly doesn't model the peaceful resolution of problems.

Children who bite need to be safe too
Children who bite are almost always up and walking, and the biting occurs mostly when there is too much frustration or even excitement. It is as though the child shorts out with excess energy and bites. Not good news for the baby who gets bitten, but there are ways to deal with it. If the parents present look for the signs and learn to notice what triggers the biting baby they can support them in those times. Magda Gerber relates her experience with a child who bit others in her parent-infant classes. She talked with the little boy, acknowledging his feelings and at the same time making it clear to him that biting another was not allowed. She explained that it hurt the other children and she was here to see that every child was safe, including him.

Something to bite on
Magda attached a plastic ring on a ribbon to the little boy's shirt, explaining to him that when he was going to bite, he was going to bite the plastic ring. With Magda's support noticing when the child was triggered and her reminder of the ring, the toddler learned to alter his biting habit so that no-one was hurt. He could still bite and release whatever energy caused him to bite, but he and the others were safe.

Here in Hauraki in our parent-infant classes we also had a child who caused much distress with her biting. This toddler was brought to every class by her Mum who was herself in a violent relationship, but she turned up every time because she valued the support she received for her daughter and herself. The skilful class facilitator talked with the Mum to find out ways this child comforted herself when things were out of hand. It was her dummy. She would put her dummy in and give it the works, mouthing out that extra energy.

Mindful of the story from Magda, the class facilitator and the child's mother learned to observe so well, they could see when this little girl was triggered and could support her to get her dummy instead of biting a child. With this kind of support and after two sessions, this intelligent child could recognise when she needed her dummy and would retrieve it from her mother's bag. She was 16 months old. Would that her Dad could manage his emotions so elegantly, but one can be almost sure that he did not get the kind of support as a toddler that his daughter had.

This too will pass
When you are in the thick of it with a baby or toddler you can think that things will go on forever in their favour - it feels like you will never get another decent night's sleep, that there will always be nappies, that this child is going to bite her way into school. When my daughter Clare was around three she discovered the joy of screaming. It nearly drove me spare. I had a most wise Plunket nurse, Puck Hutton. Puck gave me a wonderful piece of her wisdom in support: *"Pennie, have you ever seen a bride going down the aisle in nappies, screaming, with her dummy and cuddly? No? Well this too will pass."*

Sleep

What part of sleep don't you understand Babe?
How many parents have wished for knowledge of the spell that sent Sleeping Beauty into a deep sleep? It's true, you probably wouldn't want to do the hundred-year version of the spell, but if only you could get the baby to sleep long enough and at the right time, wouldn't that be magic? That way you could get some precious sleep yourself.

Space age parents, stone age baby
The way humans do things has changed a lot since babies were designed. For tens of thousands of years babies were carried for at least their first year - the *in arms* period - and that is where they slept. In many cultures that still happens today. Even in the western world there are parents returning to this

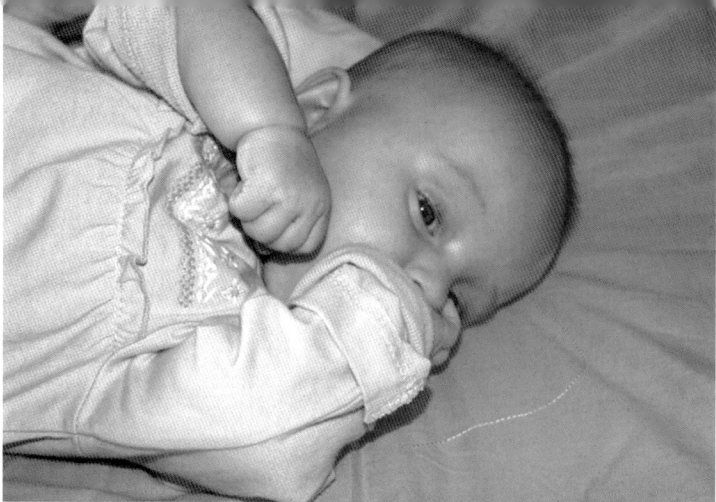
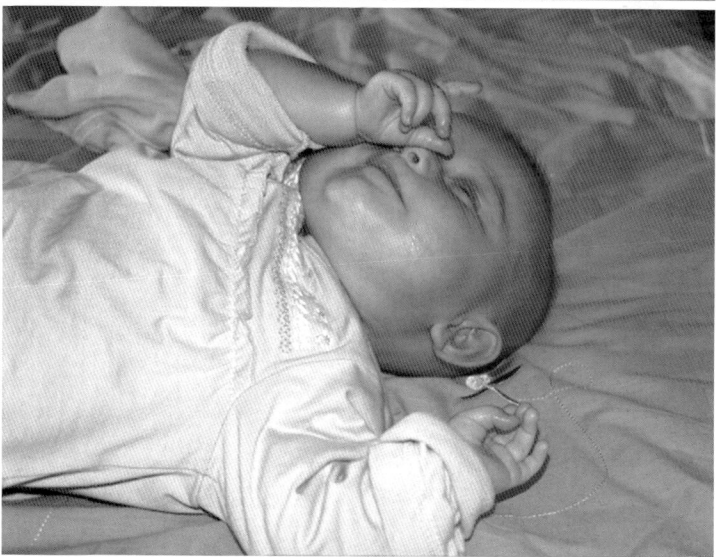
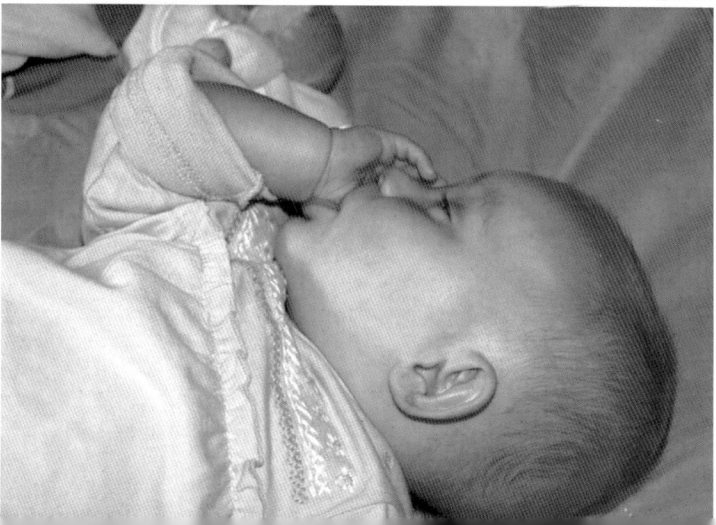

approach. These parents carry their babies rather than put them into prams or baby-buggies, and their babies do what they did for the nine months they were growing in the womb: they sleep on-the-move, soothed by their mother's movement, her voice, and not least, her relaxed state of mind. These babies feel safe in contact with the mother's body, her heart-beat and the rhythm of her breathing; safe enough to drop off to sleep with ease.

For crying out loud!

Sleep is one of the biggest concerns for new parents, and partly because somewhere along the line we have picked up versions of 'The Sleep Story' that might need upgrading. We already know how important the story is in deciding the outcome, and there are some very dodgy stories circulating about babies and sleeping. 'Crying it out' or 'controlled crying' are two stories that would have you believe sleeping and crying go together. You only need to ask how you yourself would like this approach to realise it's probably best not recommended for babies.

Which sleep story?

When it comes to bed time, there are two main versions of the sleep story for babies. The first is sleeping in the parents' bed, or in their bed-room if not in the same bed. In this story, the baby is comforted by the breathing and close presence of the parents. In the second version the baby sleeps in his own bed in his own room. Be honest: not too many of us would choose to sleep in a room all by ourselves when the person we most loved and trusted in the world, the one with whom we felt safe and comforted, was in the next room. Why do we think babies and children would choose differently if they had a choice? But which ever sleep story you choose to act out in your home, there are some things to keep in mind to make it work for you and your baby.

Relax and tune in

Everything we have learned about heart coherence applies to the sleep story. A baby is not going to go to sleep with ease if he is uptight or upset - neither do you. If, as the senior dancing partner, you are calm, your baby

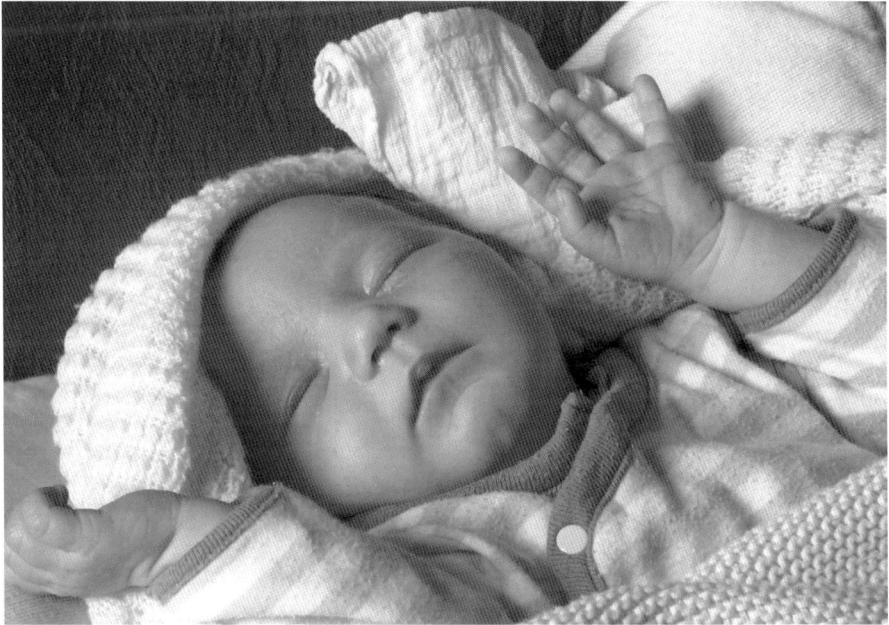

will match your frequencies and calm down as well. That's the first step: relax. If you haven't done it already, start to listen to the 'talking' your baby does before she cries. Parents and grandparents have, for tens of thousands of years, listened in and worked out that the different sounds are the baby's own language. That is how the baby tells you what's up for her, and if you don't get it, she has to shout more loudly. We call that crying. Australian researcher Priscilla Dunstan says the 'word' *(infant vocal reflex)* *"owh"* indicates your baby is tired. If you listen in you'll get to recognise your baby's 'words' for hungry *"neh"*, wet or discomfort *"heh"*, discomfort of lower wind *"eairh"*, need to be burped *"eh"*, and contentment. When you can understand what your baby is saying it's easier to be relaxed.

Routines: the rhythm of your dance
I know we dismissed the word routine earlier on, and we replaced it with 'care moments', but regular rhythms are extremely important for babies. Humans are creatures of habit, our reptilian brain loves the rhythm of

routine. Think about it: do you have a favourite chair or place on the couch where you always sit and you get quite peeved if someone else parks themselves there? Do you always sleep on the same side of the bed? Do you always hang the sheets on the line the same way? Babies are humans so it follows that routine works for them too. Routine gives their world some predictability and that counts for a lot when the whole world is new and strange for them. Routine and predictability help them feel safe. Routines build up their trust in the world and the people in it. It may be that your baby has already established a sleep routine but it isn't the one that you want. Well relax, routines can be changed, gently and surely, and in surprisingly little time.

Different rhythms, different dance
Around the world different people have different sleep routines for babies. Different routines yield different rhythms by which babies ease into the world of sleep. Throughout history feeding-to-sleep at the breast has been the all-time favourite, and feeding-to-sleep is being practised by more and more people - including those who bottle nurse. If nursing to sleep is the

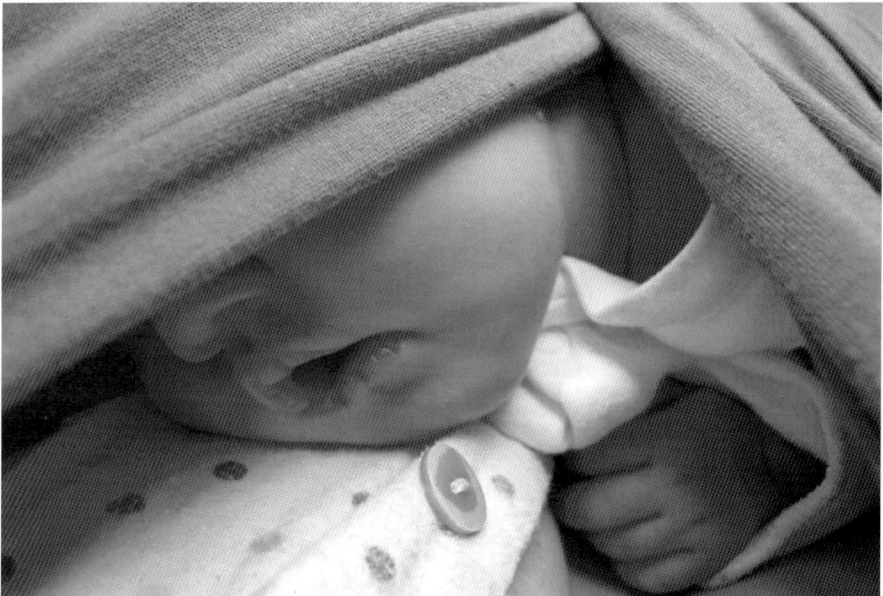

routine you and your baby choose you might get some strange looks from people who hold a different sleep story, but that is their prerogative.

The rhythm of the breath
Being in a room where a baby can 'follow' another's breathing is a big factor in his sleep safety, as well as a way to lull him into the world of sleep. Your breathing is as familiar to your baby as your heart-beat. He was lulled by both rhythms before he was born, and he listens out for them in his first years, particularly in that first year. He tunes into the rhythmic sound of your breathing, and it is as if it leads him in his own breathing. Sitting with or beside your baby, and focusing on your breathing is another way to ease a baby into sleep. As you relax and slow your breathing, your baby follows you.

What are your thought habits?
Remember, you are the one who stays calm and grounded and when you have read your baby's words and signs that he is tired you begin your routine. You won't start by 'wobbling around' thinking thoughts like:
   I sure hope tonight isn't a repeat performance of last night.
   If she doesn't stay in bed tonight I'll scream.
   I wonder how long it will be before you cancel my night's sleep?

Thoughts are energy, and thoughts like these are certain to knock you out of heart coherence; they guarantee the exact results you don't want. You will have heard the saying, "What you give out you get back", and it applies to this situation too. This is the Law of Attraction in action.

You choose
Choose gentle confident thoughts which match what you want to happen and communicate them to your baby in a gentle and sure way:
   It's almost your bedtime and I am going to change your nappy before bed.
   You look very tired, it won't be too long and you will be able to sleep.
   Are you ready for one last drink?

If you follow a routine in your words and actions your baby will very soon learn to anticipate what will happen in her sleep routine. This is more of that predictability which is so important to her. Treated as your partner like this she will surprise you with her cooperation.

Abandoned

Every child's biggest fear is the fear of being abandoned because abandonment means death. Most adults aren't that keen on the idea of abandonment either. Those of us who have woken up in hospital after a procedure will remember that it wasn't a great experience even though we were old enough to reassure ourselves that we hadn't been abandoned. A young child can't do that. That is why the Pikler Daycare Centre in Budapest ensures one of the parents **must** be there when his or her child wakes from their first sleeps at the daycare; that is part of their settling-in process. That is the way parents build their child's trust, instead of destroying it.

Where am I?

Maybe somewhere in your party-animal youth you had the experience of waking up and not knowing where you were and if you did, you will remember that too was not a good experience. So when a baby goes to sleep on his mum and wakes up on his mum, there are no surprises, it is predictable. Predictable feels safe and the baby knows he hasn't been abandoned. When a baby nurses himself to sleep and is placed into his bed, that too becomes predictable, especially when the parent listens for the waking sounds and is there to greet him child as he comes into wakefulness. And for those following a different sleep story: when you put your baby into his bed to fall asleep you assist him in establishing his predictable sleep routine, and he too knows he isn't abandoned.

Your baby leads in the sleep dance

The baby is the only one who can learn the skill of going to sleep and turn it into a habit. You have already worked this out, but I'll say it again: No-one can make anyone else go to sleep. Your baby is the only one who can get himself to sleep. So now that you have your baby ready for bed, gently place him in bed on his back, and speak to him in that same confident, calm way. You might like to put your hand very gently over his heart area as you speak. When you are calm, this calm touch, along with your soothing words, works really quickly in establishing heart coherence for your baby, *I'll leave you now and let you have the rest you need.*

And when he cries...

By now you know his cries, and there is crying and crying. The crying that is escalating does not do your baby any good at all. It raises the levels of the stress hormone cortisol in his body and that affects his whole system. So if your baby goes beyond the whimpering cry, you can reassure him with your presence until he gets this new habit of falling asleep in his bed. Remember, when your baby can't see or hear you he thinks that **you** have disappeared altogether. That is pretty scary when he has been used to being in you 24/7. It might be enough for you to reassure him:

I am still here, and I will be here when you wake up.

I know you can put yourself to sleep, and I will be here when you wake.
And you listen for his waking and you are there to greet him. When you are as good as your word, you grow his trust.

If babies get really upset - (and remember this is a physiological state that they have gotten into with too much adrenalin and cortisol floating around in their little bodies, it's not them playing you up as some people would have you believe) - they can't get back to heart coherence without you as the tuning fork. They can fall asleep in the state of stress and exhaustion and there are some people who advocate that, but it is hardly the way to nurture a partnership or build trust between the two of you. What you can do is put your hand over their heart area and talk them down:

I am here and I can hear that you are upset.

I trust that you can calm yourself down - and keep the soothing talk up until they do.

I know that you can fall asleep all by yourself - and stay with them until they do.

Gently does it

Habits take time to get established. If you have gotten into the habit of driving around the block to get your baby to sleep that probably took a few car trips to become a habit. Trust that your baby is easily clever enough to learn a new sleep habit if you dance the same routine with him until he has the steps off by heart. And remember, Life itself isn't static, so don't be surprised when established sleep routines morph and change over the months. Growth spurts, teeth-aching-gums, big emotional changes, unwellness... these Life events will alter your child's rhythms, including their sleep rhythms. And yours. Console yourself knowing that when your baby is a teen you'll hardly be able to prise him out of bed.

Food glorious food

Food should always be a pleasure

When I attended the Pikler training in Budapest the sessions on food began with Emmi Pikler's dictum that food should always be a pleasure. At that moment I knew Emmi Pikler had a very different take on food and babies from my mother. Mum was in charge of the food and very nutritious food it was too: all of it organic, all fresh out of the garden, fresh from the farm, nothing out of tins, and all of it prepared and served up appealingly. Emmi Pikler and Mum had the same idea about the quality of food for babies. It has to be the very best. It is the raw material for building the precious brain and body of your baby, so of course it makes sense to feed him *real* food, natural molecules which his system recognises and can use as the building blocks for Life.

Who's in charge?

Where Mum parted company from Emmi was that Mum thought she should be in charge. Like Emmi did, Mum decided what we would have, but unlike Emmi, Mum decided how much we would have, and that we would eat all of it - no matter how long that took, and no matter if the meal descended into a grim kind of warfare. Whether we needed it or not was beside the point, and whether we *wanted* it or not didn't even come onto Mum's radar. The natural appetite we were born with - the apparatus which lets us know when to eat and when to stop - was very quickly rendered superfluous to requirements. The sense of alienation, reinforced each meal time, was an even more serious side-effect. It permanently affected the relationship making it anything but a partnership. And all because Mum didn't know how to dance the food-partnership dance.

Your little gourmet is capable and wise

It is useful to revisit the stories which support babies and partnerships when considering baby's mealtimes. Capable and wise babies can tell you when they have had enough, though you will have to learn to read the sign language. Tiny babies push food out with their tongues, they turn away from you and the spoon, or they push you away with their hands. If you truly believe babies are capable and wise, respect them and what they are telling you.

Your little gourmet is a free and equal human being

Free and equal healthy human beings are not forced to eat. Neither are they cajoled or tricked into eating more than they have indicated they want. They do not have their hands held tightly while food is spooned into them because babies use their hands to sign to you they don't want anymore. By holding their hands you are effectively saying that what they say does not count. Free and equal human beings decide when they are ready for each mouthful, they do not have food 'shovelled' into them. If you need an alternative to shovelling, try this, it works like magic: Hold the spoon up at your baby's eye level about thirty centimetres from her face so she can see what is about to happen next. Keep holding the spoon there, waiting, and your baby will open her mouth when she is ready. Magic. She participates in the pleasurable food-partnership dance.

Highchairs are containers

Free and equal human babies are fed on the lap so that the close, warm relationship established during breast feeding or bottle feeding is allowed to continue and flourish. Meal times are times of pleasure and intimacy and children who are lap fed look forward to these times in the same way they look forward to snuggling up for a story. Even when children have the necessary skills to get down from the lap and eat at the table, nearly all of them choose to linger another month or two until the drive towards autonomy gets the better of them. If you are wondering how on earth you manage to feed on the lap and you have more than one child, take heart, it can be done. The nurses in Budapest had eight babies to care for at one time, and it worked beautifully for them.

Silly talk

Having learned to read what your baby is telling you at mealtimes, what will you tell them? Children aren't picky eaters by nature. They have to be taught to be picky eaters; we teach them with the words we use about food:

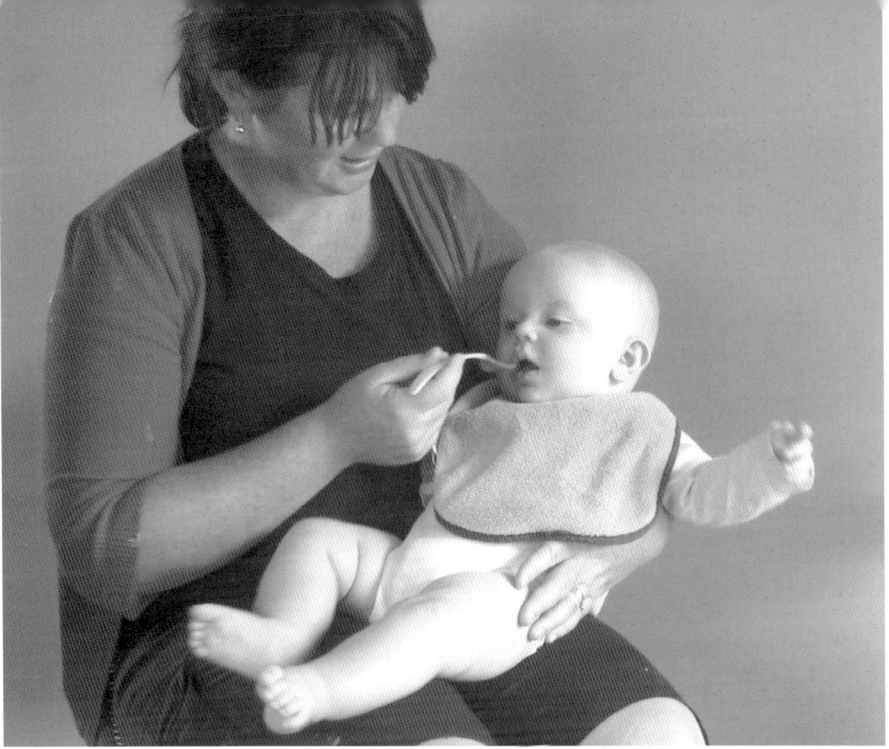

Don't you like it?
Do you like pumpkin?
You don't like avocado do you?
I don't know if you like cauliflower?
I won't give you any parsnip, you don't like it.

There will usually be one or three foods that a child doesn't like, but let their taste-buds be the decider. Don't you go putting the idea into her head that she doesn't like celery. It's also odd that it is only vegetables and other food we deem to be 'good for them' that we refer to in the negative. I haven't heard too many parents saying things like, *"You don't like apple-pie do you?"* Not unless they were being sarcastic knowing full well apple pie was a favourite.

Finished?

When a child is fussing with her food what you won't say is "Stop playing with your food." That is a silly story to sell to children. It seeds the idea into the babies' minds that food is for playing with, when in fact the fussing is their sign language that they have (probably) had enough. Playing with food doesn't even occur to them unless you instil the idea when you misread their cues. Taking your cues from your baby's fussing you ask, "Have you finished?" If your baby hasn't finished she will resume eating.

Partner talk

If she has finished she will give you some cue that lets you know that she doesn't want any more. You will acknowledge her communication, *"I see you have finished so I will take the plate from you. It looks like you enjoyed it."* Babies treated respectfully like this know that you are in tune enough to read their sign language and so they feel understood. They know no-one is going to force them to eat, so mealtimes are a great source of pleasure to them. They relax around food, eat when they are hungry, and eat until they are replete. This sets them up for life with healthy eating habits.

Not one spoonful more
Despite any lingering fears you may have about your baby starving herself to death, babies treated like this do not starve themselves because food is such a pleasure for them. Emmi Pikler's story which was used to train the nurses at her institute is *"Not one spoonful more."* Ever. Nurses never tried and sneak that 'extra spoonful' in when the baby or child had indicated they had had enough. For more than 60 years people at her Institute followed this story and in that time not one child ate less than they needed to maintain their health.

Chew your food
Most of us are aware that we ought to chew our food more thoroughly than we do. Thorough chewing breaks the food down into a mush and mixes it well with saliva; the saliva in the mush begins the digestive process. Humans have teeth designed especially for grinding food to the required mush - molars. Anywhere between 12 and 19 months old your baby will get four molars, and their arrival signals that your baby is ready for food that needs to be chewed. Not before. In other cultures parents have chewed the food to start the digestive process and then fed the chewed-food to the child. If you're not too keen on that idea get yourself a mouli or a sieve. Sieve or mouli the food to get it to the consistency of well chewed food. That makes it easy for your child's digestive system to extract the nutrition from the food instead of passing it through in chunks with all the goodness wasted. There is a popular trend to give babies food that ought to be chewed well before those babies have the right teeth to do that. Be kind to your baby's tummy. Buck the trend, 'mush the food' and wait for the molars.

Call a truce, declare peace
The child who refuses to eat, who refuses to be defeated in the mealtime battle, will almost certainly be the child who hasn't been asked into partnership. This child is expected to dance to someone else's tune rather than being encouraged to move towards autonomy. It seems that quite unconsciously, these children have to find ways to exercise their autonomy as it pushes to develop, and eating, toileting and sleeping are three very good

places to start. When any of these activities start to resemble a battle ground it is time to reassess the battle plan. Call a truce, declare peace, take your cues from the child and get back into heart coherence. Battles around these three crucial activities do long-term unnecessary damage to the psyche. As my Dad used to say, *"There is no such thing as an unwounded soldier."*

Toilet talk

Poos and wees

In cultures that more closely follow the choreography for the bonded parent-infant dance than we do, there are no nappies. The mother and baby are so in tune that when the baby is *about* to empty out, he signals his need, and his mother understands and holds him out with a cue (e.g. *Psss*). This nappy-free practice is not about 'toilet training', it is being bonded and responsive to each other. Infant and mother are in high-level coherence so the adult can read the subtle cues and anticipate. This Elimination Communication can be practiced as early as the newborn time, and can be as simple as catching the first wee when your baby wakes, or noticing the expression and noise that signal the need to poo. Practiced with respect, this can be pleasant and fulfilling for your baby and you. But if you choose not to take this path to nappy-free, there are a few things it is useful to know so that you can work through this area of your baby's development in partnership.

Nappies aren't forever

Remembering Puck's advice that this too will pass, how do you deal with the period of toileting without turning it into a battle? Firstly, your baby needs to have reached the stage where he knows he is a 'me' (an autonomous being) and he knows about 'mine'. You will know when he has reached this stage because he can talk about himself in the first person - that is, he can refer to himself as "I". Babies must reach this stage in their autonomy before they can consciously navigate themselves through successful toileting. If you start earlier than this you can achieve 'no nappies', but it comes with a heavy price in your baby's psyche because it amounts to forced toilet training. Wait until your child starts referring to himself as "I".

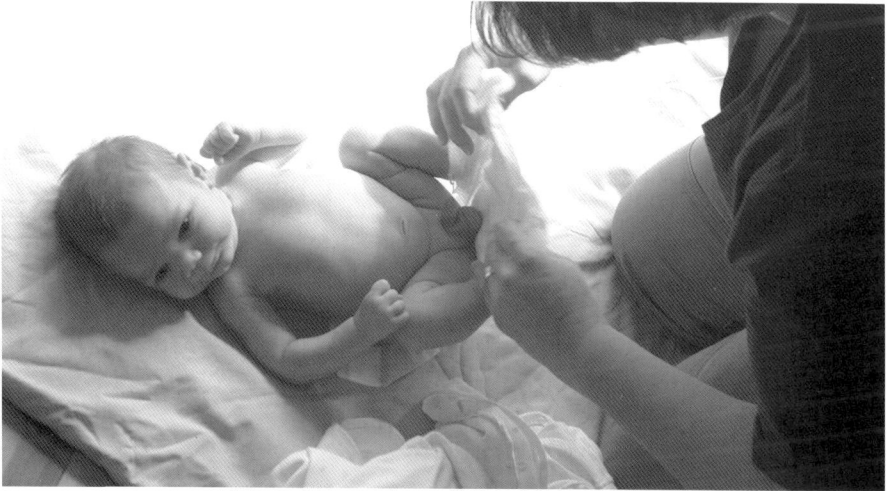

1 2 3 wee

Then watch for these stages: It begins when they tell you they have already toileted, this is the first step. They have to know, consciously, that *they have done it*. There is no way babies can skip this step even though you might wish they could have told you earlier. Next they tell you *while* they are doing it in their nappies. As frustrating as this might be for you, recognise the progression. Now your baby's conscious bodily awareness recognises the process *as it is happening*. A baby has to be aware of having done it, then of doing it, before he can recognise and act on the more subtle sign of *wanting to do it*.

Ready, set, go

Now is a good time to introduce the pot. If you are observant, you will notice that your baby gets a shock when he first becomes aware of passing a poo in the potty. He may even be very upset. Pikler observed that all babies have what she termed, 'the poo poo shock'. After that first poo that he is consciously aware of, he may reject the pot for days, even weeks. Reading his sign language you will wait, knowing that the drive for autonomy will override this shock before too long. Then your baby will resume toileting and it will be accomplished easily, without a battle, and without long-term psychological damage.

Will

Holy Will

Will has had a bad press in our culture in relation to infants and toddlers. It isn't commonly seen as a Holy quality in a child; but rather as a nuisance, an obstacle to be overcome, a defect in the design, or even something to be broken. If you think this last phrase is too extreme, consider many times have you heard baby battlers say the following of a baby or toddler:

You have to show him who is boss.

Don't let her rule the roost.

It's either you or him.

There is something very lopsided about these statements; they are not about partnership. None of these statements treat the parent-infant relationship as a dance of two equal wills. Sure, the adult is older with more experience and is therefore expected to lead the dance of two wills, but not to scuttle the dance altogether.

You're on your way

When you treat your baby as a partner and invite her into the dance you are already giving her the chance to exercise her will in the way it needs so that it can grow. When she chooses the timing for the steps she is using her will to cooperate. She learns to give you her hand when she is ready, to open her mouth when she sees the spoon, to lean forward when she decides to have her nose wiped. She is getting to exercise her will, which like any 'muscle', needs to be exercised and grown. From very early on, say 12 to 15 months, your baby can choose from two (and only two) tee shirts, or the two pairs of pants that you hold out when she is dressing. She is learning that she has some say in her world, and she can't reach independence without this knowing.

Enter will

So what about tantrums, those virtuoso displays of will by toddlers? This is where the Holy comes into it: Holy as in sacred, sacred as in worthy of awe and respect. We have talked about how every child is programmed to explore the world at all cost, how every child is made to learn. They are pure learning-beings, building up a body of knowledge of the world. Once they are upright with their hands free, they are off. You will have noted how single-minded they are, passionate scientists, exploring anything and everything. Enter will.

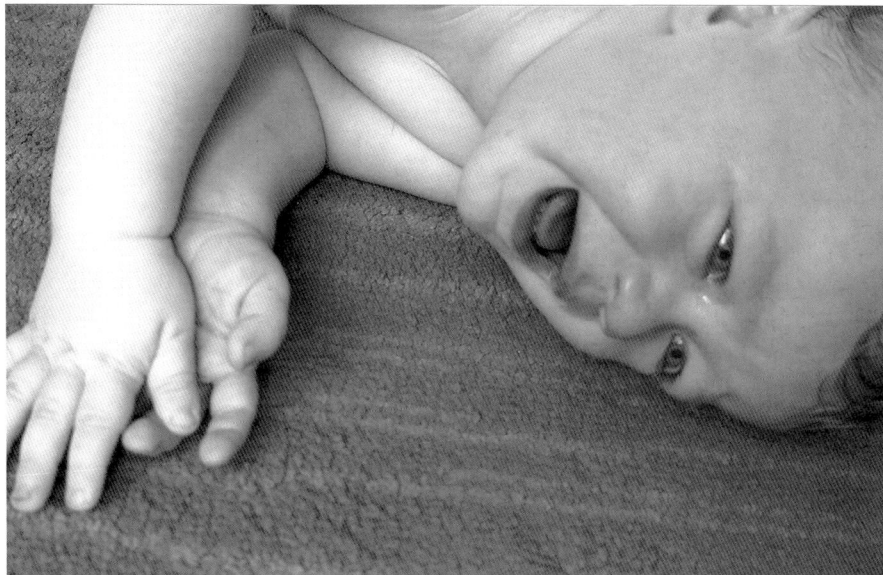

Will power

Will is a gift in the child, a piece of learner-design brilliance. Will is the power that the child has which takes them over when they meet an obstacle to their sacred task of mapping in a body of knowledge about the world. People think that toddlers can turn it on and off, but they can't. It's an energy response to an obstacle in their path as passionate learners. It is designed so that they have the energy to overcome obstacles and get on with discovering what they had in their 'single-mindedness'. When you understand that, you don't take it personally. You stop seeing it as a power play against yourself and you find ways to work around it.

Are you the obstacle to learning?

Skilled dance partners find something equally as fascinating for the toddler to switch their single-minded attention to. That way *you* don't unwittingly become the obstacle. Put yourself in the baby's shoes, it must be hell for them when their senior dance partner becomes the obstacle. That's 'baby-catch-22'. It is also desirable, sensible even, to see that your toddler doesn't become over-tired, over-hungry, over-stimulated. These are not resourceful states for your child. She hasn't got much to come and go on in these states and will can easily take over.

A terrible beauty

A toddler in a full flight of will is truly an awesome sight, in the same way that the Irish might describe it as a 'terrible beauty'. The child is taken over by the energy called will, and it can scare the wits out of you if you don't understand what is happening for the child. If you don't know what is happening for the child you probably won't manage it in a way that is healthy for your child, for you, and ultimately for our society. These early experiences around an energy as fierce as will imprint deeply in the child, affecting his self-view and his view of the world.

Dancing posture and stance

Just as there is the right stance and posture for the tango to be marked highly by dance judges, there is a more effective stance and posture in the Dance-of-Two-Equal-Wills. It is much better to have the effective posture off pat before your infant-turns-toddler and reaches the full-on-take-over stage of will where you will need all of your skills to match theirs. Infants and toddlers are marvellous readers of energy and the subconscious. Any child with red corpuscles in their blood is going to make a run for it when they meet the energy of the hands-on-hips adult because the posture is about confrontation, and it is all shaped up on the adult's terms. There is nothing in this stance which asks for cooperation and partnership.

The invitation to dance

The palms up invitation gesture offers something very different. It *invites* the child to be a partner. It allows them the courtesy of deciding whether they will dance or not, it gives them the chance to exercise their will. Very importantly, it gives them time to work through their emotions as they make their decision. Watch this story unfolding: it is the classic negotiating story of two equal wills. You will see the needs of each partner being expressed, and as in any negotiation you will see offers placed 'on the table', you will see compromise and resolve, and a win-win outcome.

The dance of two equal wills
The toddler has a block he is interested in and he has been carrying it around. The senior partner sees the block and wants it back in the box which has been put away. The senior partner is busy holding a younger child having just fed him, so she holds out her hand in the gesture of invitation. The toddler sees the gesture and interprets it correctly, though it is clear he is not *willing* to give the block back. Yet. He walks up to the adult but moves away again. He is not ready to give up his needs. After considerable inner turmoil, the child picks up a plastic lid and puts it in the adult's hand. The adult, without a word, places the lid beside her and continues to hold her hand in the gesture of invitation.

The child focuses on the hand, delays some more, and eventually puts the block, not in her hand, but at her feet. The adult does not make a big fuss that the negotiations have been concluded successfully, that both parties have danced elegantly. Neither does she say cutting things like: *"Well you took your time with that one didn't you? Next time in my hand. You knew very well I wanted it in my hand."* The senior dance partner has her block back, which is what she wanted. The toddler saved face by putting it back but in a location of his choosing. A tender stroke on the child's cheek was the adult's way of telling the child that the relationship was still very much intact after an emotionally charged negotiation.

The Invitation Gesture

I invite you to put this book down for a couple of minutes and try this out for yourself. You will get a sense of what your baby feels when it comes to cooperating with you - or not. If you can invite someone to do this experiment with you, sitting opposite you, even better.

Try the first posture, the palms up invitation gesture.
(You don't need to sit cross legged.) As you do it, take some time and notice how it feels in your face and your body. Notice what happens to your breathing and notice how you feel. Your baby will read all of that.

Now try the second posture, the hands-on-hips gesture.
Notice how it feels for you in your body. Once again, notice what happens to your breathing and how you feel. Your baby reads that too.

If you switch between the postures you will notice what your body does with the different gestures. Be sure, your baby notices too.

Imagine someone wanted you to give them something and they were doing the invitation gesture. How would you feel about cooperating? How would you exercise your will? And how would you feel about cooperating when faced with the second gesture?

Palms up

The palms up gesture works like magic, in all sorts of situations. Use it every time you are offering something to your child, when you are waiting on your child, when you want something from her, when you would like her to cooperate with you over dressing or wiping her nose. The message given to a child who needs her nose wiped is very different when you use this gesture instead of the more commonly used approach. Commonly, the child has her head held from behind so that she cannot get away, and her nose is wiped whether she is ready or not. She cannot exercise her will. There is no opportunity for it when she is caught clamped between the adult's hands. That's why, bright girl that she is, she takes her opportunity when she sees you *want* to clean her nose and makes a run for it.

You're not the boss of me

You have to give it to her, she knows power-over tactics when she sees them. She resists unless it is partnership that she is offered. Children, when they get more language, express it beautifully when they announce, *"You're not the boss of me"* but this sort of battle of wills is very wearing and unhealthy. Try instead the palms up gesture. Parents and childcare workers tell me using this simple gesture has astonishing results. It makes all the difference in their relationships. It ends the battle and furthers the partnership. Try it for yourself. Your child will definitely notice your new dance step and join you in the heart.

Back to the future

Children are our future

I know it is stating the obvious, but children are our future. What children themselves need for a rosy future is a bonded relationship, first with their mum, and then with dad and the rest of the family. As a country we need to look at the policies we are enacting that affect small children. We need to fund the services which support the first relationship; services like domiciliary midwives, visiting Plunket nurses, visiting district nurses, Parents as First Teachers and parent education. As I write, these services are being pruned in favour of institutional childcare.

Is the bottom line money or children?

This very recent arrangement of institutionalised childcare suits the state and the business world, assisting as it does with the country's skilled labour shortage. But since when was money more important than our children? *"We can't afford it"* is the loud cry when extended parental leave is mooted. *"We need two incomes to survive"* is the parents' lament. But what if parents had a choice? What if central government policies supported the family bond by investing in parent education and parental leave? It comes down to political will. Steve Biddulph cites Sweden as an example: when parents were offered extended parental leave, childcare rolls dropped overnight. When 'the economy' comes before children and families, the very fabric by which the economy exists (people-society) starts to unravel.

Crazy stories

Most parents don't want to sacrifice their children's childhoods on the economic altar, but many can't find a way around it given current policies. Those parents can feel it in their hearts though. Handing their children over to 'experts' does not feel like the right thing to do, yet they succumb to the pressure from every direction; workplace, in-laws, friends and very often even from their own partners. They ignore their heart intelligence, leave the child, and then they rationalise to live with their decision. Magazines have not helped. Super Mum stories have glorified the few women who, with million dollar make-up, manage to balance roles of Domestic Goddess, Business Goddess, Culinary Goddess on one finger and never drop an olive on the polished tiles. Stories about Super Mums who have chosen motherhood as their career for their children's early years are scarcer than cloth nappies on washing lines.

Choice stories

Then there is the story of women and choices. This is a very hard-won chapter in the generic stories of "Partnership", "Capable" and "Free and Equal". Women have rights, including the right to choose. In relation to mothers with small children, a woman has the right to choose mothering or paid employment. All well and good, but where is the choice for the mother who has no choice but to seek work simply to put food on the table, let alone pay a mortgage? More worrying still; what choice and rights does the baby have? Or is this chapter still waiting to be written?

Spaghetti for brains

Another prevalent story in the media which justifies the leaving of babies is that small children are very poor company. Stories of this genre would have it that if you spend most of your time with small children your brain will turn to mush. Granted, spending time with small children might not be everybody's cup of tea, but this is not a true story. Children definitely cannot turn your brain into mush. We just made that story up so we'd feel better. If you spend your time with your child in the heart you will be surprised just how much you learn, and just how much you grow your head and your heart intelligence.

Job stories

Many parents worry that they will not be able to advance in their careers if they take time out to spend those first years with their babies. Very often these are the same people who took years out to do their OE and yet they slotted straight back into employment when they returned home. Time out for OE or time out for your babies, in terms of being absent from the NZ job market there is no difference. For your baby though, there is the world of difference. Three or four years are but a sneeze to adults, they just fly by. They are a lifetime for your baby, and they set your baby up for her lifetime. Invest in those early years. You can never get them back and you won't ever regret putting your baby's development and relationship first. Trust. These are times when there is a shortage of people who show initiative, and who just plain turn up for work. There will be a job there waiting for you.

Who's looking after your baby?

Remember, they download *everything*

Throughout this book we have looked at your central role as 'the known' in your baby's life. It's not what you *teach* your baby that counts, it is how you *are* with him or her. As Joseph Chilton Pearce says, *"We tell children how to be and they keep mirroring back what we are."* Children less than six years old learn by observation. Effortlessly they download the example of who you are, how you behave and interact with them, and with others. These programs are all imprinted into the subconscious at lightning speed. This raises big questions for us as parents, questions about ourselves and our behaviour. Is this the behaviour I want my baby to imprint? Equally, it raises questions about the environment. Do these behaviours and environments promote heart coherence and growth, or are they incoherent thereby damaging and stunting growth? These same questions come into sharp focus if you have to leave your child in the care of others.

Babies, money and politics

If you are lucky enough to live in a country like Sweden where children are a priority for politicians, you won't need to find someone to care for your child for at least sixteen months. You will be paid parental leave in line with the research on infant wellbeing. Most of us reading this won't belong to countries where children come first. That means you probably *will* be looking for someone to care for your baby when you go back to paid work. Even so, do what you can to put this off as for long as you can. In Slovakia they pay parental leave for the three years that constitute infancy. Very few parents can manage the ideal of three years, but if you possibly can, do what it takes to be with your child for at least that first crucial year.

If not you, then who?

Remembering that it is the relationship that is the *most* important thing to consider, you might have a family member or friend who can offer safe, 'respect-full' in-home childcare for your child. In-home childcare can be as informal as that, or you can make a formal contract with any one of the in-home childcare agencies that operate nationally. In the formal arrangements your child will be with one adult and up to three other children. A widespread myth has grown up about in-home childcare with many believing it isn't as good for children as centre based care. This belief is partly based on the idea that children 'need to learn' and pre*schools* will "prepare the child for school", and partly based on the education sector's insistence that young children need a 'trained teacher' to succeed. They don't.

The best preparation for school and life is being one half of a warm loving relationship, where the child and adult hang out together **talking**, laughing, singing exploring.... From that place of emotional safety the child can venture out and make warm friendships with others. The young child doesn't need too many 'others' because too many relationships overwhelm him and put him into that dangerous cortisol-stress overload where, among other things, it is impossible to learn. The next best preparation for school is to have unlimited time for uninterrupted play. The more play, the more brain growth, the more learning, and more building of that firm foundation required for school-learning. Children can experience warm relationships and warm friendships in home-based care in the more natural setting of a home and a garden. A child who spends many hours in care is deprived of

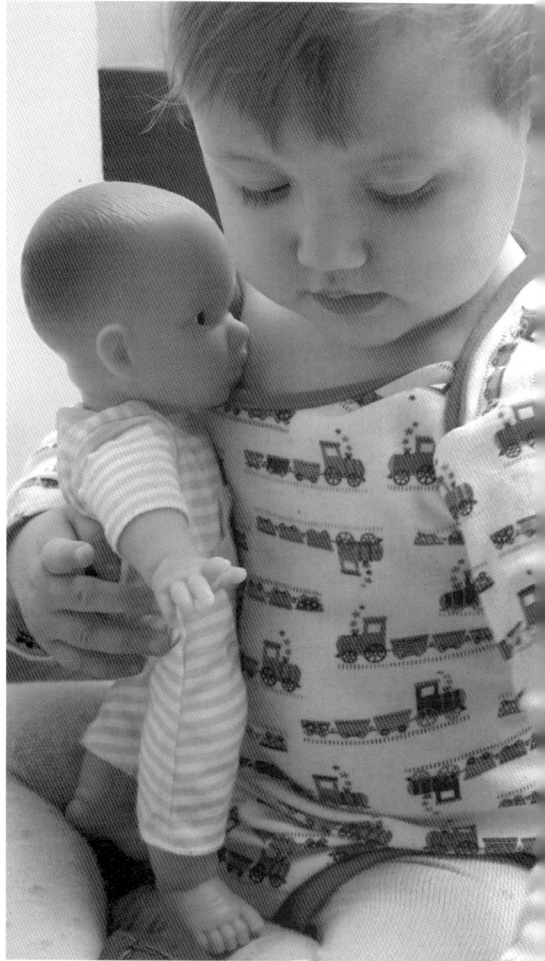

her home life and home-based care can fill that deep need. Of course you would meet the caregiver first and judge if who-she-is would be a good fit for you and your baby. And if the answer is yes, then you would proceed with the period of settling. Read on...

Choosing a childcare centre

If parents decide for centre-based care, it will be one of the most important decisions they make for their children, so it is not made lightly. Even if you are a 'last minute' person, this is one decision that needs time and research. A lot of important things need to be considered if the child-care experience is going to work for your child. It will come as no surprise to you that the first and foremost consideration is the relationship. Your child has grown her trust in you, you are her emotional anchor, she feels safe with you. It's a bit like you not being all that keen on going to a concert or to a restaurant all by yourself. You are old enough and capable of managing the situation all by yourself, but you would rather take a friend, an emotional anchor. The baby is not capable of managing on her own as we noted way back near the beginning of this book. She needs emotional support to manage. Because a relationship takes time to grow, your child needs time to grow a relationship with one person at the childcare centre, sometimes referred to as the *primary caregiver*. Your child needs time enough to sense that *you* trust the caregiver, and time enough to extend her trust outward to include the caregiver. This is a period of 'getting to know you', the settling period where the child builds an emotional anchor in the centre so that she feels emotionally secure in the same way that you do with your friend at the concert. How long will this take? A minimum of two weeks, and that is why you can't leave it to the last minute.

The two hour 'romance'

Some centres take children after two hour-long visits. Few of us would trust someone and decide to spend every day of our lives with them having known them for only two hours. We'd like time to get to know them a bit better, and so would your child. The daycare centre at The Pikler Institute has guidelines for settling which I have turned into a quiz. Look for it in the appendix on pages 114 - 116. Many centres have adopted these guidelines as their settling policy, but if the centre you are considering has a different settling procedure, negotiate with them to work with you on the important points in the quiz. They will make a world of difference for your child.

Go for the Love Story
Look for a place where they act out the Love Story, and use your heart and your instincts to help you. It's not enough for centres to *say* they are based on the principles and practices of Emmi Pikler or Magda Gerber as many do. As Emmi Pikler said, this is not a dogma. This is not a matter of simply words or principles, it is the appropriate spirit behind the actions that is of importance. People who adopt the right spirit act out the Love Story.

What to look for in a centre
The privatisation of childcare has resulted in a huge variation in the quality of centres, right through from centres where the practice and the settings are truly exemplary to the sadly-just-scraping-through-as-legal centres.

So how do you choose? I would listen to what they *say* they do, and then I would observe to see if they do as they say. Because the most important criterion is the quality of the relationship, take time to observe interactions carefully. You need to know in your heart of hearts that this adult will be a sensitive partner for your child, offering a safe respectful heart-centred partnership dance. One look at how centre staff feed and change babies will tell you if you have found a suitable place to leave the most precious 'thing' you are ever going to be responsible for.

Dysfunctional is not fun
Observe the relationships between the staff. Does this feel like a harmonious team? Just as there are dysfunctional families there are dysfunctional teams of teachers. Make sure you look carefully at the group size because too many children sharing a space is the biggest stress factor for children in care. Check out the group size for the older children in the centre too. Some centres keep the group size for babies at or below the ideal maximum of twelve, and yet they have two year olds in groups of forty-plus. Would you like to spend your time in a room of forty two year olds, or even twenty five two year olds? Thought not, and neither would your child. This really is just baby sitting. It isn't quality care or education.

Rigid or accommodating?
Watch to see whose timetable the centre adheres to: is it the roster-timetable or is it the children's inner needs? Centres that feed babies when they are hungry and sleep them when they are tired are centres worth seeking out. Look for peace and harmony. Invariably when people visit centres which are acting out the Love Story they ask, *"Where are all the children?"* The children are all there but it is calm and peaceful, a place of heart coherence. Sure, there is upset every so often, but only every so often, not constantly.

Getting ready for school
Personally, I would be ultra wary of any centre that advertises itself as 'getting your child ready for school'. This is a marketing phrase playing

on parents' fears that their children might fail and be left behind. Early childhood has far more important things to achieve than 'knowing your colours and writing your name'. This is the critical time for learning to make friendships and becoming literate in the complex web of people skills. The ability to get along with others in all sorts of situations is a better indicator of future wellbeing, happiness and success in life than knowing how to add or read before seven years of age. People master people-literacy most easily in early childhood through their play. Play gives plenty of opportunities to learn skills for negotiation, conflict resolution, leadership, teamwork and more. Look for a centre where the teachers see their role as supporting children to get along with others, a centre that doesn't rob children's childhood-play time by setting out school-like activities.

Home and garden

Lastly, your child will get to school soon enough. What your child is missing out on by being in care is a home life and time outside in nature. Many centres are working to make their environment more homely and less 'schoolly'. If you can choose a centre that looks, smells and functions like a home with a garden rather than a school with a playground, your child is in for a very enriching time while you are away at work.

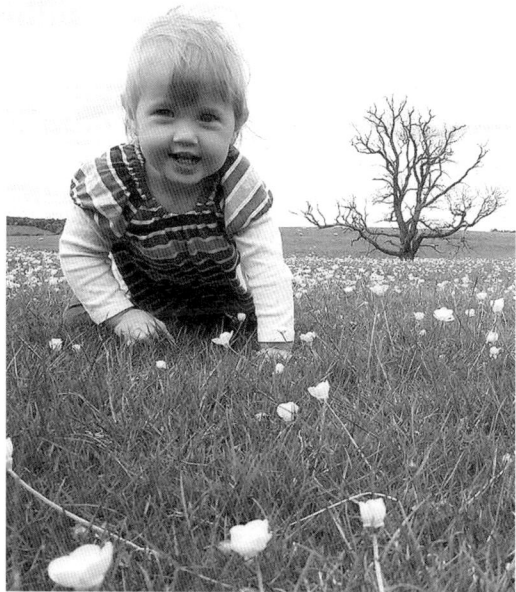

> Nature is not a place to visit. It is home.
> *Gary Snyder*

Dancing in the heart

The model is everything

I started this book with a story about my Mum and how she got it right third time lucky. But Mum got off to an even worse start when she was born in 1924. Mum was Nanna's fourth child and her sister Kura before her was so desperately ill as a baby that Mum's arrival was 'the last straw' and Nanna had a breakdown. She threw baby Peggy out of her bed. Peggy was given to friends of the family to look after for eighteen months before Nanna was well enough to have her back; the very months in which it is critical to make a partnership, the months when Peggy would have imprinted baby nurturing.

The peace dance

I can't say for sure, but it is unlikely that Nanna had the kind of support which helped her grow a partnership with her babies. I was lucky, I had Puck, our wonderful Plunket nurse. Puck lived in her heart, and with her few wise words she taught me that it didn't matter how much I knew in my head, it was where my heart was that mattered. My Mum on the other hand had been given the kind of help which filled her head. The head is only half of the story. It wasn't until Mum declared peace and softened into her heart that she had the success she had been striving for all along. Paradoxically, it was her baby who led her there. Mum did what every bonded mother has ever done, she took her cues from her baby. Take your cues from your baby and together you will dance in the Heart.

The heart is the hub of all sacred places, go there and roam.

Bhagawan Nityananda

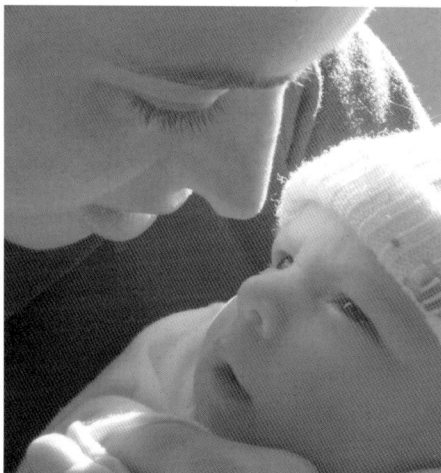

Dancing in the heart, toddlerstyle

New steps

Since this book was first published, many parents have contacted me with the same story. The partnership ideas explored within these pages worked like magic for them with their baby, but when their baby walked confidently into toddlerhood, their new-found parenting confidence started to unravel. They began to lose their peace and calm, their heart coherence shifted into incoherence. Resulting skirmishes escalated into toddler-battling in spite of parents' intentions to keep the peace. These parents intuited there had to be advanced steps for dancing elegantly with toddlers, but they weren't sure where to find them.

Terrible Twos
Many people hold a very low opinion of toddlers, calling them names like 'the terrible twos' and claiming they need to be tamed. Implicit in the titles of many books written for parents of toddlers is a struggle for power: "Toddler Taming: A Parents' Survival Guide", "The Toddler Discipline Solution", "Taming the Terrible Twos", "Toddler Taming Tips'. From the titles, it seems the toddlers stand a good chance of winning the struggle unless the parents seek special coaching to give them the edge. But in their heart of hearts, parents know there is something wrong with a relationship where one of the partners has to be tamed. Taming is not the way to nurture any child's unfolding spirit.

Check the use-by date
For centuries most cultures have been embedded within the power dynamic of **domination** where the defining question is, *Who is going to win and who is going to lose?* Winning and losing is okay for rugby and the Olympic Games, but not for your relationship with your toddler. The dynamic of domination has its roots in child-rearing practices, and it carries within it the seeds of every kind of abuse, including child abuse. It originates from within our ancient reflexive 'fight and flight' brain complex. At this time on our planet there is an urgent need to replace the outdated dynamic of domination in our child-rearing, in our education, as a way of doing business, and in our relationship with the environment.

Time for a new dance craze
The question giving rise to the very different dynamic of **partnership** is, *How can we cooperate so we both win; so we both have our needs met?* Activating this power dynamic is dependent on us making a conscious decision, and then staying aware of our behaviour. In making the choice for partnership, consciously, we operate from the higher more evolved system in the brain, the part that works in unison with the intelligence of the heart. (You'll remember the heart has its own brain linked into our prefrontal cortices.) Working out how to use our personal power in ways that teach our children how to partner people in the spirit of cooperation and collaboration

will be our greatest contribution to world peace. Your relationship with your toddler is the perfect place to start.

Power dancing

Your toddler is right on cue in her development. She has taken the best part of a year to realise that she herself is a person, separate from Mum, Dad and the others. Now that she is aware of existing and acting separately from others, her autonomy begins to unfold. She is ready to learn how to stand in her personal power and use it. As we noted earlier, will and power are incredible forces, and learning to harness them with elegance will take your child some time. While she is learning how to handle her personal power, the way *you* handle *her* will decide which one of two power dynamics will become her 'relationship template': domination or partnership?

Partnership step one: Yes or No?

Up until now you have been using the gesture of invitation because all partner-dances start with an invitation. What you might not have realised is that when you offer the invitation gesture, your child has two choices. As a dance partner, she can accept or decline, she can say 'yes' or 'no'. Up until now, your child has accepted your invitation, but unfolding autonomy has delivered her to a new place. It's as if she says to herself, *I've been saying 'Yes' to the invitation all these months, what will happen if I say 'No'?* And she tries it. She learns that a lot happens; *No. No. No!* It becomes a firm favourite, a kind of toddler anthem. *No!* It gives her an instant experience of personal power, and the satisfaction of making her own choice. Indeed, it is the experience of making her own choice that is so powerful. She has discovered something that will hold true for the rest of her life: following her own intuition and making her own choices is a right-use of personal power. But these are early days in her power-journey and you are her coach when it comes to modelling right-use of personal power alongside others.

Partnership step two: Yes or Yes?

Your toddler wants to choose, she wants to do it her way, and she wants to feel the power of that. (Don't we all?) When the yes-no choice you are offering no longer results in the two of you working together, offering the invitation with a yes-yes choice rescues you both from a standoff. You offer the choice **complete with the palms-up gesture** that you have perfected during your baby's first year:

> *Do you want to climb into the pushchair by yourself, or shall I lift you in?*
> *Would you like me to peel your mandarin, or do you want to do it?*
> *Are you going to sit at this side of the table for your dinner, or at the end?*
> *Do you want Daddy to help you with your jarmies, or shall I?*
> *Do you want to serve yourself, or would you prefer Nanna to do it?*

With the yes-yes choice it doesn't matter which option she settles on, you are both heading in the same direction. Your child will dance this new step with you quite happily until her unfolding delivers her to yet another new place in her quest for autonomy - a place much the same as the place you are in.

Great expectations

Imagine you were writing an email and you were in the middle of a sentence. Your partner (and here you get to imagine your ideal partner if you don't have one) asks you to come and give a hand with the dishes. It is extremely unlikely that you would stop immediately, mid-sentence, jump up, click your heels and head to the kitchen. You are more likely to say something like, *"Hang on a minute. I'll just finish this sentence and I'll be there"*. When humans have their interest focused on one thing, it takes some time to 'change gear' and begin a new focus. For some reason though, many parents expect their toddlers to 'snap to it' and obey their requests instantly. Children, like adults, need time to change their focus.

Trust feels like trust

Returning to the scenario of you writing an email: imagine if your partner came and stood over you waiting for you to hurry up and finish your sentence and come and help with the dishes. And what if your partner started counting, "1, 2, 3...."? I don't know about you, but I would not react with grace in that situation, and I would be nowhere near heart-coherence. If I were 'stood over' I would be more likely to carry on typing and even begin a new sentence. I rebel when people use 'power-over' tactics, and toddlers rebel too. Like your toddler, I much prefer to follow my own timing, to come when I have cleared my mind ready for the new task.

Partnership step three: Yes or Yes, plus time
Not too many toddlers can tell you, "Hang on a minute, I need some time to change my focus and deal with your invitation". Yet knowing that is what you yourself prefer, you can start offering the same courtesy to your toddler:

Your pyjamas are on the couch. Daddy or I can help you with them if you like. You let us know when you are ready.

I can see you are fascinated with Nanna's brooch. When you are finished, either put it here, or give it to Nanna.

Yes you do need your nappy changed. Bring me a clean one from the shelf when you are ready.

You need a bath before dinner. Come and let me know when you are ready to turn the taps on.

I have observed many parents (and teachers) roll their eyes heavenward on hearing about this step in the dance. They declare that their child wouldn't buy into this level of invitation, they believe their child would just ignore the request and carry on. (I did mention that as a society we have a low opinion of toddlers.) But parents and teachers who try step three report back incredulously; *It worked! After a couple of minutes she came to me with her nappy! After a short time he just gave Nanna back the brooch!* When you give your child space and time, you show him you trust him to make the partnering decision. You give him room to change focus when he is ready, to choose how he will accept your invitation, and not least, to demonstrate that he is a social being who likes to please you. On average, it will take your toddler between three to five minutes to change focus. That's about as long as it takes you and me.

Beyond the limit

As your child gets more words to play with, he enters into the game of negotiation with gusto. Negotiation is his newest game for exploring his personal power, and because it is so new to him, he isn't skilled in it. Yet. He needs lots of practice, and guess who he is going to practise with? While young children are learning the art of negotiation, they can become so caught up in the details that both child and parent end up going round and round and round. The child 'negotiates' himself into a corner from where it is almost impossible for him to shift focus and make a choice. Help him out, help him break the stalemate.

Partnership step four: the stalemate

Throughout this dance with your child, you are the senior dance partner, so when the dance is going nowhere and it needs to reach a conclusion, it is time for you to take the lead. The stalemate situation that results when children can't make a choice signals it is time for you to lead and state the choice again:

Your choices are a banana or half an apple. Would you like me to choose for you?

Your red jersey is clean, so is your turquoise jersey. Shall I choose for you?

Be prepared to be surprised by how easy this can be. Very often your child will just say, *"Yes"*, with relief at having had an easy way forward presented to him.

The third option

Sometimes toddlers and young children end negotiations by choosing an offer that wasn't even on the table; they choose to wear their yellow jersey. If the third option results in you both heading in the same direction, accept the offer as any capable negotiator would. Some parents ask, "But aren't they getting their own way?" like it is a bad thing. It isn't about getting your own way, although as a parent, you make up all the choices so it could be said you are getting your own way most of the time. If it helps, think how intelligent your toddler is when he thinks outside the square and settles on other options to keep the dance going.

Partnership step five: managing a stalemate

And be prepared for the child who digs himself in deeper than that. Stalemates very often occur when time is the determining factor. There isn't time for the child to choose with leisure. The challenge then is for you is to assume the role of the senior partner in order to keep the partnership alive. You need to step-up mindfully, or otherwise either you - or your child - can move in as the dominator instead of a partner, and the dominated will be left wondering how and when all their personal power drained away. When offering the choices to manage a stalemate, be mindful that you might well be required to 'choose one', so make sure that one of the choices you offer is something you can carry out gracefully.

> We have to go now. Your choice is to walk with me to the car, or I will carry you. Choose now or I will choose for you.
> You can have a bath with Mummy or with your sister. If you haven't chosen by the time I find you a towel I will choose for you.

And then you make your choice, and keeping to your word, you kindly

and firmly carry out that choice. Note that 'firmly' does *not* mean rough-handling. It means you breathe, stay centred in your decision, stay centred in your heart, and you keep your resolve.

And the referee's decision is final
Your child might not like your choice, he might even protest, loudly. As long as you are kind yet firm with him, over time he'll begin to realise that being a social being also means fitting in with others. He will start to understand it is better to make his choice while it *is* still his choice. He will learn that as well as you being kind and firm with him, you don't bear a grudge or hold onto stuff either. You don't rub his nose in it when his behaviour isn't very elegant, after all he's just getting his balancing act with strong emotions sorted. (Have you sorted that one yet?) He will also learn that you are as good as your word, and that puts a net of safety around the relationship. The very act of giving clear boundaries provides your child with a predictable container within which to perfect his skills of living and loving with other people. So gently, and kindly, stick to your word.

Expect what is possible from your child, no less and certainly no more
Many of us embarking on the journey of parenting have had little or no experience with small children, so we have little or no idea what to expect. Often we can expect behaviour from an eighteen month old that is way beyond her developmental capabilities. Just because a child is up walking and talking doesn't mean she has mastered self regulation of her emotions and her will, nor that she will be compliant to all of your demands - or even some of them if her blood sugar is low because she missed a snack. All learnings take time and these are huge learnings.

It takes a village to raise a child and to support that child's family
Children in general, but toddlers in particular, spark the chance for *us* to undertake huge learnings, and not only about the right use of power in a partnership with someone who is vulnerable. We ourselves have body-held-memories of power-battles from way-back-when that we haven't dealt with. When our toddlers 'push our buttons' and stir those memories, they offer

us the chance to heal the energy and the subconscious memory. Focusing on the heart and the breath can usher us into a place from which to practice partnership, a place where we can 're-parent' ourselves. For others of us, that which is triggered is too big to manage alone. When it is too big, pluck up the courage and seek specialised support from someone in your village. Every old flaw that is healed is one less to pass on to your children.

Dancing freestyle

In the dance world, 'freestyle' means choreographing dance steps into creative combinations for new situations. In the parenting world, when you add the four new steps into your existing repertoire you can't help but progress. With practice, you will very quickly learn to combine your many partnership skills into creative combinations to suit each situation with your child - and to stay in heart-coherence while you do it. That is real progress, not just for you and your family, but for the whole human family as well.

Appendix 1 · Toys for brainy babies

Imprinting variety in 3D

Your baby is learning about this three dimensional world, and the 'toys' that help her to do that are much more likely to come from your kitchen cupboards, a garage sale or the beach than from a toyshop. The greater the variety of things she plays with, the more she learns about this world, and the greater the number of connections she makes in her brain.

Who does the work?

You want your baby to connect his brain cells, so choose toys where he does all of the work, choose toys that do nothing at all by themselves - no batteries, no remotes. We buy that stuff because 'we've seen it all' and we need novelty. Babies, however, are fascinated by bowls, pine cones, paua shells, wooden pegs, blocks...

Imprinting beauty and nature

After young babies have discovered their hands, they go on to explore the different objects you make available to them. Remembering that babies imprint everything, choose beauty and not junk. They will also need plenty of beautiful natural materials if they are to download the patterns of nature. See if you can avoid plastic toys altogether - with three exceptions: Lego, dolls and balls.

Scientists, architects, mathematicians and magpies

As the months pass babies begin putting things into things. Next, they graduate to putting the things that are the same inside each other like the stacking cups and bowls pictured. Around the same time they are fascinated with stacking things on top of each other - building. When you provide collections of things that are the same or similar, your baby will get busy sorting, classifying and gathering up collections like a little magpie. Help her out by providing her with enough things to collect, and with buckets and baskets to put her treasures in.

Above: First toys for babies, 'toys' that will fascinate children into toddlerhood.
Below: Stones and stainless steel for hours and hours of learning and play.

Above: Wooden blocks from the Childspace workshop in Wellington.
Below: Wooden play objects, most of them from Trade Aid.

Above: Miracles of design and colour from the beach.
Below: Engineers, architects and builders begin their apprenticeships here.

Appendix 2 · The culture of kindness

Facing ourselves

Do you know someone who does something repeatedly and they don't know they are doing it? They aren't aware of their habit, it doesn't show up on their radar. Or conversely, do you know someone who doesn't do something but they swear they do?

> *"I always put my clothes out in the wash. Honest. And I always hang up the towels."*

Most of us are just as sure we respect our babies, we certainly mean to. But maybe when we shine a light on our habits things look a bit different.

I invite you to find a pen and do this short quiz.

Have you ever? Would you like it?

Answer each question honestly - simply circle yes or no.

Yes/No	Have you ever picked up a baby or a child from behind?
Yes/No	Would you like someone to pick you up from behind?
Yes/No	Have you ever picked up a baby or a child without telling them?
Yes/No	Would you like to be picked up by someone who didn't tell you they were about to pick you up?
Yes/No	Have you ever picked up a baby or a child without asking them if you could?
Yes/No	Would you like to be picked up by someone who hadn't asked you if that was OK?
Yes/No	Have you ever picked up a baby or a child without waiting for them to accept your invitation?

Yes/No	Would you like someone to pick you up before you agreed and were ready?
Yes/No	Have you ever wiped a baby's nose without telling them?
Yes/No	Would you like someone to wipe your nose without telling you?
Yes/No	Have you ever put a hat on a baby or child without asking them if you could?
Yes/No	Would you like someone to put a hat on you without asking if they could?
Yes/No	Have you ever put a baby or child into a carseat without telling or asking them?
Yes/No	Would you like someone to put you in the car's seat and do up the seat belt without warning or invitation?
Yes/No	Have you ever taken a sweatshirt off a baby or child without first telling them?
Yes/No	Would you like someone to take a sweatshirt off you without first asking you?
Yes/No	Have you ever taken something out of a baby's or child's hand without asking them for it?
Yes/No	Would you like someone to take something out of your hand without asking and waiting for you to give it up?

Something doesn't add up

Now that you have answered the questions, you will probably notice two things: Firstly, all (or most) of the grey shaded questions are circled 'Yes', and all (or most) of the unshaded questions are circled 'No'. Why is that? Why is it okay to treat a baby one way, while at the same time we would not like any of it done to us? Are babies not human? Are they not the same species with all of the human sensitivities and emotions? Of course they are, so the mismatch doesn't make sense.

Stories are powerful, especially hidden stories

The other thing you may have noticed as you were answering the questions is that you may have had stories in your head as to why you did or did not invite baby to be picked up, or why it was "stupidity to ask a baby to give something to you, because what if he swallowed it and choked?" *Hearing* these stories alerts you to our culture's subconscious stories around babies and children. And it is good, because it means your **un**conscious habits are up on your radar screen when you notice your stories. When they are up on your radar you can revise and upgrade the stories, but you can't do that when they are hidden. Unpicking the stories we leaned growing up in our culture is an important step toward the Culture of Kindness.

Got any ideas?

The bit to really wonder about is why there is such a mismatch of what we *think* we do and what we *actually* do. Why is there such a mismatch in our behaviour - respectful for adults, and disrespectful for babies? It is all new for this baby, she has no idea what is going to happen in this game called life. Will her Mum and Dad be life coaches, and respectfully let her know what is going to happen? Will they respectfully invite her to be part of the Partnership Dance, or will they 'just pull her up onto the dance floor' without warning, and expect her to keep up?

> There is no single effort more radical in its potential for saving the world than the way we bring up our children.
>
> *Marianne Williamson*

Appendix 3: Settling quiz for parents & teachers

Write your score for each question in the box alongside.

Group size is a major factor for stress in babies and children - and for the economics of childcare. Yes, it is legal to have 20 babies in a group, but that is an economic consideration. It is not a consideration for babies' welfare.

1. Is the group size in the room between 4 and 8?   **15 points** ☐
2. Is the group size between 9 and 14?   **10 points** ☐
3. 15 or more?   **0 points** ☐

A child in care is a child in separation from her parents, and separation is super-stressful at any age. 'Settling' is the process of transferring trust to another, and as in all relationships, the settled relationship takes time.

4. Is there a Settling Policy that is given to parents on enquiry? **5 points** ☐
5. Do parents know that the settling process will take a **minimum** of 2 weeks?   **10 points** ☐
6. Does the parent visit with the child for short periods to begin with, short enough so that there is **no** care procedure required, for example, changing nappies or feeding?   **15 points** ☐
7. When the length of the visit is increased, does the parent change the nappy in the presence of the child's designated caregiver, with the caregiver looking on?   **20 points** ☐
8. Does the caregiver do her first 1-3 nappy changes with the parent looking on?   **15 points** ☐

This is the time when the parent and caregiver begin to make a deeper relationship and the baby knows this. She knows the 'family' is being extended. During this time the child witnesses the transfer of the parent's trust to the caregiver. This is a critical part of establishing a safe place for the child: 'If Mum or Dad can trust the caregiver, I can too'.

9. Does the child's first sleep at the centre happen during the first week of the settling process?   **Subtract 20 points** ☐

10. Does the child wake from her first sleep in the
centre to the caregiver?   Subtract 20 points [ ]
11. Does the child wake from her first 2-3 sleeps in the
centre to her parent?   20 points [ ]

> *Sleeping is the hardest part for the baby because she loses consciousness and wakes to a new world. As adults, we are disorientated waking in an unknown place, let alone to unknown people. Even though the sounds, surrounds, smells in the centre are unknown to the young child, the face and the voice of the parent is known. The parent's presence is a major factor in the child's learning that this new space is part of her expanding world.*

12. Does the centre ensure every child has a primary caregiver? 20 pts [ ]
13. Does that caregiver have a 'buddy', the person the child will
learn to trust next as her 'care family' expands?   15 points [ ]
14. Does the primary caregiver stay with the child until the end
of infancy which is 3 years of age?   15 points [ ]

> *One caregiver assumes the role of the substitute primary caregiver from the parent. This designated caregiver is initiated as the child's **emotional anchor** in this new setting, and **ideally** until the child is three. (It's a little bit like our relationship with our hairdresser. We know and trust our own hairdresser but if he or she is away, most of us aren't too keen on trusting someone else to cut our hair. And that's only hair and hair grows!) When the baby gets to trust one caregiver as her 'emotional anchor' she feels safe. From this place of **emotional safety** the baby can venture out and grow relationships with others.*

15. Is everyone on the team courteous in respecting the relationship
between the adult and the baby? That is, they never interrupt the
person while she is feeding or changing a child?   15 points [ ]

> *We wouldn't interrupt if two adults were speaking. A baby is a person too.*

16. Is there a safe place on the floor for non-mobile babies
to play without being disturbed, or being used as an
obstacle course?   10 points [ ]
17. Does every baby and young child have extended time
outside in Nature every day?   20 points [ ]

Add up your score and subtract any points lost in questions 9 & 10

TOTAL [ ]

If you are a parent...

Between 180 - 205 points

This is a place where your baby's psychological-emotional wellbeing is the top priority for the caregiver and/or the team. This place will grow to be a 'home away from home' and your family will be treated as part of their family.

Between 160 - 180 points

If everything else you have seen ticks all the boxes of what to look for in a childcare setting you have found a place where your child's well being is *consciously* cared for.

Less than 160 points

If what you have observed in the centre ticks all the boxes *except* for this quiz, it may be that settling hasn't yet become a focus of practice in the place you are considering. Negotiate with the caregiver to provide the quality settling that will make the difference for you and your baby. Making these changes will benefit both your baby *and* the provider's service. If they won't accommodate your requests, keep looking.

If you are a caregiver-teacher...

Between 180 - 205

Congratulations. You have turned the fine words in the policy folders into reality. You see your vocation in childcare as a practical journey of empathy, consideration and kindness.

Lucky children and lucky families.

Between 160 - 180

You have implemented many of the important factors that add up to the psychological and emotional support a baby requires in this first separation from her family. Keep going.

If you wish you had scored between 160 and the possible 205...

You won't be alone. Until quite recently, the critical importance of settling has been overlooked by most in the early childhood sector. The quiz contains very specific points you can work on with your team. Every point you achieve adds up to greater short and long-term mental health for the babies and children in your care.

My thanks to...

Dr Anna Tardos and her team at the Emmi Pikler Institute in Budapest. Your knowledge is truly vast, as is your generosity in sharing it. Had I not met you there would be no book. It is your respectful, skilful dance with babies which has been my inspiration. You have gifted us the 'how' to dance.

Michele Fill, Sally Christie and Trish Hatfield. The dance steps I learned in Budapest were able to be adapted into our New Zealand setting because of your support, both as friends and workers for CAPS Hauraki.

Maureen Perry, Sue Smith, Regan Mayo, Samantha Claire, Gonny Ormsby, Sharon McIntyre, Fran Thompson-Stevens and Levi Sikking for allowing me to observe your parent-infant classes. Long may they continue.

Stu Guyton, Viv Shearsby and Jean Rockel, who have been rocking along for the babies for years and years, and who welcomed me into the quadrille.

Clare Caro, Kimberley Crisp, Natasha Kibble, Lisa McKimm, Maureen Perry, Marianne Hermsen, Liane Sanderson, Fran Thompson-Stevens and Sarah Buckley for your editing and comments to improve the manuscript, and to the Institute of HeartMath for proofing the heart related material.

Clare Caro for keeping me up to date with the research, reading drafts for this revision, making recommendations for clarity, and just for being you.

All of the wonderful women and the few marvellous men who have attended workshops with me. You are the ones with the babies and toddlers, you have taught me so much with your stories.

The stars of this book
The photos in this book were given by parents, aunties, grandparents and friends who love these babies, and by partners and friends who love the grownups pictured in these pages. My deepest thanks to Clare and Nick and their daughters Scarlett and Olivia, Chris and Catherine and their son

Conner, Bridget and James and their daughter Kokowai and son Amokura, Jane and Kent and their sons Lachie and Ollie, Mel and Karl and their son Jack, Natasha and Mark and their son Otis, Liane and Kimberley and their nieces Jerzy and Stella, Megan and Mike and their daughters Caitlin and Sophie, Fang and Bin and their son Hao Zhen, Warner and Liz and their daughter Molly, Agnieszka and Michal and their son Szymon, and Daisy and Chris and their daughter Poppy. Thanks to Angela Jones for the photos of the gestures, and to Sadalit for your photo of a child in a tantrum.

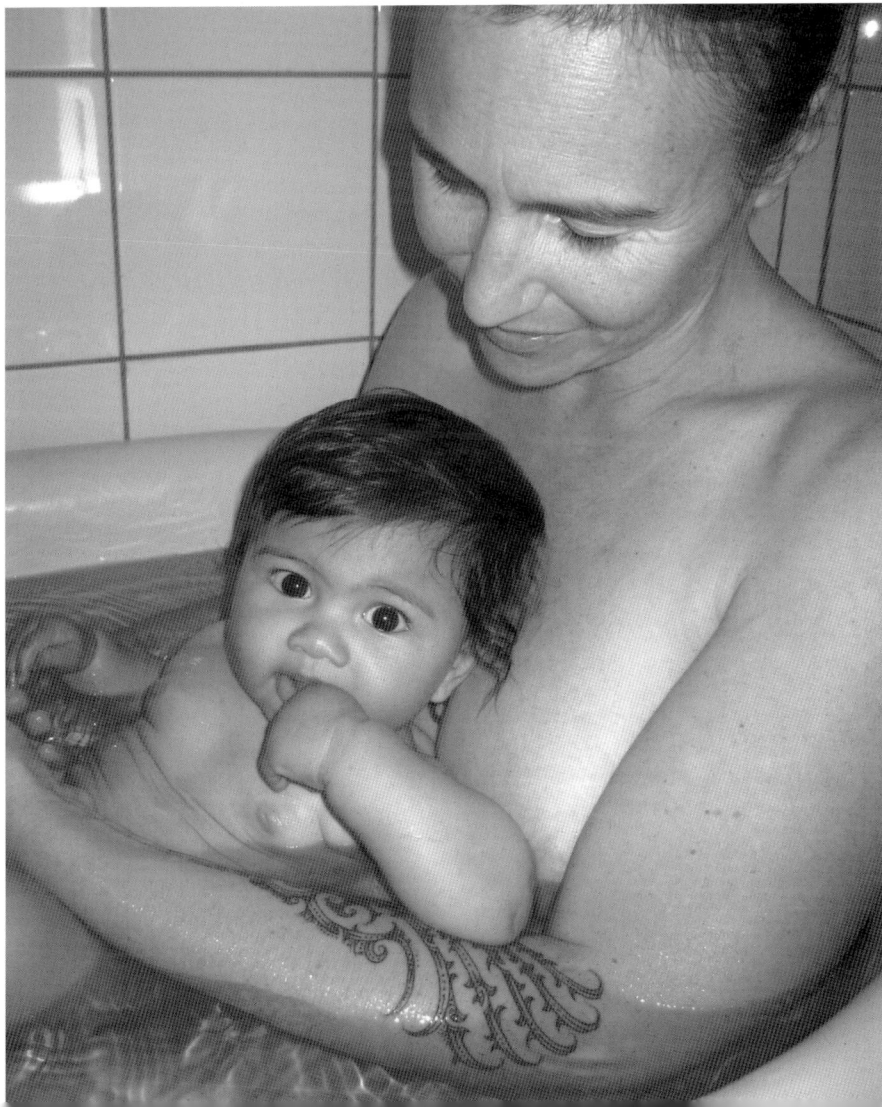

Bibliography

Biddulph, Steve, *Raising Babies: should under 3s go to nursery?*, Harper Thorsons, London, UK 2006

Gerhardt, Sue, *Why Love Matters: how affection shapes a baby's brain*, Brunner-Routledge, Hove, UK 2004

Gerber, Magda, *Dear Parent: caring for infants with respect*, Resources for Educarers (R.I.E.™) Los Angeles, USA 1998

Gerber, Magda, *Your Self Confident Baby: how to encourage your child's natural abilities from the very start*, John Wiley and Sons, New York 1998

Hannaford, Carla, *Awakening the Child Heart: handbook for global parenting*, Jamila Nur Publishing, Captain Cook, Hawaii 2002

Hermsen-van Wanrooy, *Babymoves*, Baby Moves Publications, Nelson, NZ 2002

Hunt, Jan, *Natural Child: parenting from the heart*, New Society Publishers, Gabriola Island, Canada 2001

Jackson, Deborah, *Three in a Bed: the benefits of sleeping with your baby,* Bloomsbury Publishing PLC, London, UK 1989

Leidloff, Jean, *The Continuum Concept*, Penguin Books, London, UK 1986, first published 1975

Lipton, Bruce, *The Biology of Belief: unleashing the power of consciousness, matter and miracles*, Mountain of Love/Elite Books, Santa Rosa, USA 2005

Maluschnig, Liz & Defregger, Stephanie, *Did You Know*, Delightful Books, Wanaka, NZ, 2012

Miller, Alice, *The Drama of Being a Child*, Virago, London, UK 1983

Pearce, Joseph Chilton, *Evolution's end: claiming the potential of our intelligence*, Harper, San Francisco, USA 1992

Pearce, Joseph Chilton, *Magical Child*, Bantam Books, New York, USA 1977

Pearce, Joseph Chilton, *The Biology of Transcendence: a blueprint of the human spirit*, Park Press. Vermont, USA 2002

Pearce, Joseph Chilton, *The Death of Religion and the Rebirth of Spirituality: a return to the intelligence of the heart*, Park Street Press, Vermont, USA 2007

Pert, Candace, *Molecules of Emotion*, Touchstone, New York, USA 1997

Pikler, Emmi, *Unfolding of Infants' Natural Gross Motor Development*, Resources for Infant Educarers, Los Angeles, USA 2006

Rosenberg, Marshall B., *Nonviolent Communication: a language of life*, Puddle Dancer Press, USA 2003

Tolle, Eckhart, *The Power of Now*, Hodder, Sydney, Australia 2000
Eckhart Tolle offers steps in the dance of full attention which is the key to conscious parenting, and also to enlightenment. The steps he outlines are easy to follow and come free of dogma. Look for him on YouTube.

Emmi Pikler 1902 - 1984, Bulletin Number 14, Winter 1994, Sensory Awareness Foundation, Mill Valley, CA, USA 1994

DVD
Lipton, Bruce H, *Nature, Nurture and the Power of Love: the biology of conscious parenting*, Spirit 2000 Inc, Memphis, USA 2002

Websites
The Institute of HeartMath®, www.heartmath.org
The HeartMath® Institute has many resources to help you achieve heart coherence, and will email you their regular newsletter free.

The Pikler Collection: http://thepiklercollection.weebly.com
This website presents the work of Dr Emmi Pikler in the English language. It is a collection of links, videos and articles, found and brought together in one place for anyone searching for information on Dr Emmi Pikler and the Pikler Approach.

The Pikler Institute: www.pikler.org
The Pikler Institute in Budapest, Hungary, offers two-week trainings in the English language. Contact them for information and excellent resources at **pikler-loczy2@axelero.hu**

Touch The Future: http://www.ttfuture.org/
This site is a treasure trove. In the archives you will find 'giants' including Joseph Chilton Pearce, James W Prescott, Stuart Brown, Michael Mendizza, Bev Bos, Jean Liedloff, John Taylor Gatto, Bruce Lipton, Marshall B Rosenberg... to name a few. Subscribe to the site and receive their regular newsletter free.

Index

Pennie offers professional development for people who work with young children and their families, including comprehensive *Dance with me in the Heart* trainings tailored for those who work with infants and toddlers. There are follow-up facilitator trainings to the *Dance with me in the Heart* trainings for who people who wish to take heart-based parent-infant and parent-toddler classes back into their communities.

Details of all courses can be found on Pennie's website:
http://penniebrownlee.weebly.com/
On the website you will matters of interest for parents, teachers, and student teachers who want the very best for babies and young children.
To contact Pennie by post: PO Box 69, Thames, 3540, New Zealand.
To email her please use the contact page on her website.